Also by Eileen C. Shapiro:

Fad Surfing in the Boardroom:
Reclaiming the Courage to Manage in the Age of Instant Answers

The Seven Deadly Sins of Business

Freeing the Corporate Mind from Doom-Loop Thinking

*

Eileen C. Shapiro

CAPSTONE

First Published 1998 by
Capstone Publishing Limited
Oxford Centre for Innovation
Mill Street
Oxford OX2 0JX
United Kingdom

British Library Cataloguing in Publication Data
A CIP catalogue record for this book is available from the British Library

ISBN 1-900961-52-0

Typeset in 11/14 pt Bembo by
Sparks Computer Solutions, Oxford
http://www.sparks.co.uk
Printed and bound by
T.J. International Ltd, Padstow, Cornwall

This book is printed on acid-free paper

To Ben

First Word

*The obvious path
is not always
the right path.*

*— Warren Jung,
Arizona hiking guide*

Contents

Introduction

- How could Bill Gates, college drop-out and only a few years from high school, have beaten out IBM, then considered invincible, and Apple, which at the time had the personal computing market tied up?

- How did Barings go from great British institution, to almost out of business, to subsidiary of a Dutch bank – all in a blink of the eye?

- What made Dutch electronics giant Philips N.V. enter a whole set of media businesses, which in turn led to losses of hundreds of millions of dollars and finally the decision to bail?

- Why did Lloyds of London, once the master of risk management, become the victim of major risk bets gone wrong?

- Where have all the Triumphs gone – not to mention the entire British motorcycle industry?

- What ever possessed Nissan management in Tokyo to name its first sports car for the US market the 'Fair Lady,' a disaster narrowly averted only because one of its California-based employees physically pried the 'Fair Lady' nameplates off and replaced them with '240 Z,' Nissan's internal designation for the car?

- How could the German automobile manufacturers not have figured out the next target of the Japanese car makers would be one of their prime export markets: luxury cars aimed at American buyers?

- How did the great Japanese financial institutions find themselves saddled with vastly overvalued loan portfolios, thereby following in the steps of their illustrious American counterparts?

- Why did Nestlé in Switzerland and General Foods in America fail to pay attention to the gourmet coffee craze in the US market until their upstart competitors were well entrenched?

- And if Bill Gates is so damn smart, how did he almost miss the Internet revolution – even if he is now set to dominate it?

At the most basic level, the answer to all of these questions is the same: the damage was due to one or more of the Seven Deadly Sins of Business.

These are the Sins. What makes them deadly is how benevolent and helpful they all sound. Odds are, your organization is committing one or more of them. The question is: do you know which ones?

1   Terrific plans
2   Outstanding products
3   Play to win
4   Turbo-charged employees
5   Workplace sizzle
6   Learning organization
7   Forward intelligence system

The first three are the Sins of Strategy. When they are committed, even the smartest and best trained managers will inadvertently get their economics working against them. The second two are the Sins of Organization. Committing them turns a company's workforce into its worse liability. The last two are the Sins of Information. Companies committing these two find that the data they need play hide-and-go seek or other nasty tricks, often with disastrous consequences.

At first blush, you might write off the examples I posed earlier as exceptions. But they aren't. Look around you. How often have you seen smart and capable people making knuckle-headed decisions – sometimes with remarkable consistency – and wondered why? Wrap some context around the sins, and you'll begin to see the common element uniting all of them: the power of beliefs.

With the extra words, the annotated Sin List looks like this:

- *The Sins of Strategy*

    ◦ Sin #1: Trusting in your terrific plans … even though you have lost sight of what your real strategy is.

    ◦ Sin #2: Reinvesting in your outstanding products … while the market is moving in a different direction.

    ◦ Sin #3: Focusing on playing to win … when in fact you're playing the wrong game by the wrong rules.

- *The Sins of Organization*

    ◦ Sin #4: Assuming a team of turbo-charged employees ... while short-changing the investments needed to build workforce judgment and skill.

    ◦ Sin #5: Focusing on workplace sizzle ... but neglecting to provide the motivation that matters.

- *The Sins of Information*

    ◦ Sin #6: Taking pride in being a learning organization ... even though key decision makers are unable or unwilling to see the facts for the creed.

    ◦ Sin #7: Investing in sophisticated forward intelligence systems ... while consistently falling backward in the battles that count.

Here's how these sins work. Business proceeds by action, each action aimed at achieving a purpose or outcome. But, as Harvard Business School Professor Howard Stevenson points out, all purposive action is based on prediction, what we expect to happen if we do one thing versus another. All prediction, in turn, is based on how we see the relevant facts. Finally, how we see the facts – and, indeed, the facts we see – turns on our beliefs, ideas that are so deeply and strongly held that they feel like The Truth, and not like the assumptions, preferences and hopes they really are.

And that's the crux of the matter. When beliefs go wrong, then even people most passionate about making 'fact-based' decisions will find that they have been seduced by the allure of one or more of these sins – and not even know it. That creates a doom loop, bad thinking leading to bad outcomes.

Not convinced? Think about cross-word puzzles and mystery novels. Unless you're a whiz at word games, you may, on occasion, have found yourself stumped, only later to discover that the word you put in 35-across was incorrect, and therefore gave you the wrong starting letters for 36-down and 37-down. Nonetheless, once you had inked in 35-across, you began to regard it as part of the solution set, rather than as the working hypothesis it really was. Or take mystery novels. A well-crafted book of this genre provides all the facts required to identify the real murderer – but gives you the facts in such a way that you are seduced into incorrect beliefs. Then, when you turn the last page, the real mystery is how you could have missed the evidence that the author placed in plain view before you. (A great example of the genre: Agatha Christie's *The Murder of Roger Ackroyd*.)

Companies commit these kinds of sins all the time. Mercedes was sure that no Japanese luxury car could rival its own automobiles, and so saw no need to create a preemptive strategy before the Lexus rolled into showrooms across North America. Philips was convinced, based on its awesome record as a hardware provider, that it had the people, knowledge, and mentality to compete in the fast-changing media world when this was not, in fact, the case. The big coffee guys thought that most people in the US would never trade up in price to get a better-tasting brew, and therefore didn't pony up to the more expensive Arabica beans that give gourmet coffee its kick and flavor. Nissan executives in Tokyo were certain – despite urgent requests from the company's US rep for a 'power' name like 'Lion' or 'Tiger' – that a good British name like 'Fair Lady' was perfect for the company's new roadster. All these beliefs felt right. And all of them were wrong.

The answer doesn't lie in seeking to abolish beliefs, however (though one can imagine having fun by creating some deliciously bogus new fads – TFM, 'total fact management', for example, or ZBC, 'zero-based cognition'). Quite to the contrary, life – in or out of corporations – would be impossible if we didn't rely on the guidance our beliefs provide. Then we'd be paralyzed, having to begin anew with every decision, big or small. Rather the solution requires a difficult kind of balance: the ability to act consciously – to continue to make decisions based on current beliefs while finding ways to identify, test, and if need be, modify the beliefs in question. And that in turn means converting covert certainties to explicit – and therefore, contestable – assumptions.

Rapid shifts in the environment make this goal of conscious action more difficult, of course. And it is true that we are in the midst of tremendous change, with all the attendant uncertainties that such massive change brings. But lest you think that working and managing within such a context is unique compared to the relatively stable and placid times of generations past, I invite you take two steps back in time.

First, imagine the working life of a young Viennese who began his career in business in 1927 and retired in 1977, and the changes he would have witnessed over the course of career. To list a few: he would have taken his first full-time job when Vienna was rocked by violent discord and massive economic deprivation only to be propelled into the great worldwide depression of the 1930s; he would have been born at a time when the Habsburg monarchs still were in place, participated in the selection of the country's elected officials, and later watched as Engelbert Dollfuss, the Chancellor, was assassinated in his offices in 1934 by Austrian Nazis and then, four years after that, as his country was incorporated into Germany's Third Reich. During World War II, he would have first been on the winning side, and then, on the losing side. In the post-war era, he would have lived in a heavily damaged city, occupied and ruled by the Allies for a decade, and then would have participated in re-building both his city and his country.

At the same time, think about the changes in technology during his working life: the television, the computer, the transistor, and the integrated circuit would have been invented; telephones and automobiles would have gone from quasi luxuries to ubiquitous appliances; multi-day ocean voyages would have been replaced by multi-hour flights; and medicine would have taken giant strides in almost every disease class, especially in infectious diseases such as polio, pneumonia and tuberculosis.

Now shift in time and space, and imagine an American entering business in 1857, shortly before the start of the US Civil War. He would have lived through a quantum shift in the basis of the country's economy in both the north and south, especially after the abolition of slavery. He too would have experienced mind-boggling advances in technology that we take for granted today: the invention of the telephone, the electric light, the phonograph, the radio, the Bessemer process for making steel, the automobile, the diesel engine, the airplane, vacuum tubes, rapid transit, and mechanical refrigeration – all with profound effects on the content and process of business. Robert C. Post, president of the Society for the History of Technology, goes a step further: 'The late nineteenth century was the greatest period of technological change in terms of things that affected huge numbers of people's lives in basic ways – much more so than today.'

Of course, there is one group of people who had the luxury of working during a long run of prosperity and relative stability: those who participated in US businesses just after World War II, or what I think of as the 'bubble generation.' Think about the structural advantages: the US had most of the world's gold, the basis of the worldwide currency system, and much of the world's remaining productive capacity. We also had a huge, relatively homogenous domestic market that was bursting with pent-up demand and, as Europe and Asia rebuilt their economies, growing export markets as well.

Given this environment, it may have been easy to think that the challenge of change was optional; after all, when you start the game with most of the chits, you can make errors of fairly large proportions and still have good odds that you'll end up with pretty nice numbers on the bottom line. And perhaps this is one of the reasons that the business literature coming out of the US focuses so much on change. Because, in a way, for us change has been a shock, the more so because our beliefs about the innate superiority of our products, people, and policies took such a beating once our perceptions caught up with reality.

This decidedly unfashionable view of change leads to the three premises on which this book is based:

- The first premise is that the essence of the manager's job continues to be as it has been for at least a century: to make difficult decisions, intelligently, in environments of continuing and unpredictable change. You may call this leadership if you wish, but I say having to make decisions with incomplete data about how the future will evolve is just part of the job in business, and not some fundamentally new condition of today's environment.

- The second premise is that change is a constant, but that not everything changes either at once or at all. Rather change is lumpy – a combination of shifts, some of which are predictable and others wholly unexpected, and which come upon the world in a mix of gradual increments and abrupt leaps. That means that all people in business, and especially managers, have to think – about what to change and why, and what to leave as is or allow to evolve on its own.

- And the third premise, and focus of this book, is that the enemy to making good decisions in such environments is not change *per se*, which is just a fact of business life, but unchallenged beliefs, which are a matter of managerial choice. Your job, wherever you are in your company, is to bring these beliefs from unconscious 'Truth' to conscious assumption, and then to challenge, test, and modify them as necessary.

Theology has its own rules, but when it comes to the seven deadly sins of business, it makes no difference if the offenses are committed by omission or commission; real people in and around the company still get hurt. For this reason, each of the seven sins gets its own chapter in this book. And each of the chapters is dedicated to the same set of issues: How to tell which of the sins is being committed by your organization. How to be able to see the damage being created before it's too late. And how to determine what can you do about it – and what you are willing to do.

• • •

'How could I have been so far off base? All my life I've known better than to depend on the experts. How could I have been so stupid, to let them go ahead?'

That's what John F. Kennedy asked after surveying the wreckage of the spectacularly unsuccessful invasion his administration mounted at the Bay of Pigs in Cuba.

Irving Janis thinks he knows the answer. According to him the problem stemmed from 'groupthink.' Joel Barker, taking a page from Thomas Kuhn, attributes such blunders to faulty 'paradigms.' And Arie deGeus uses the term 'mental models.'

But I think Pogo, a possum who used to grace the funnies pages in newspapers across the States, put it best. His take went like this: 'We have met the enemy … and he is us.'

Beliefs make no distinctions between valedictorians and class oafs, nor between presidents and janitors: they impel to action, with effects that may make the smart look stupid and the slow look wise. What they will do for you and your organization is up to you.

Eileen C. Shapiro
The Hillcrest Group, Inc.
Cambridge, MA 02138
eshapiro@mba1981hbs.edu
or
103132.165@compuserve.com

The Sins of Strategy

At a meeting of CEOs of American hospitals, the old adage about misery loving company was proved once again. One after another, the participants shared heart-felt concerns and troubling war stories; about how short-sighted payers and bureaucracy-loving regulators were crushing their respective organizations' abilities to deliver quality care to patients, conduct first-class research, and train the next generation of physicians. One after another, that is, until one of their number, a nun whom I'll call Sister Mary Margaret, rose to speak. This is what she said:

> *Gentlemen, no margin, no mission.*

Though many people think they know how to bring their organizations into compliance with Sister Mary Margaret's dictum, they often stumble on the fundamental questions: what game they're really playing, with what ante, and how the game and its rules might or will change in the future. Which is also where the Deadly Sins of Strategy come into play:

- Sin #1: Trusting in your terrific plans ... when you have lost sight of what your real strategy is.

- Sin #2: Reinvesting in your outstanding products ... while the market is moving in a different direction.

- Sin #3: Focusing on playing to win ... at the same time that you're playing the wrong game by the wrong rules.

Missions vary. Some organizations optimize for financial returns for equity holders, others for community returns for a broad range of stakeholders. Some are in the game for the money only; others thrive on fun, the pure joy of making a scientific discovery or technical breakthrough, or the pride of facing a challenge and excelling beyond all expectations. But one thing is constant: unless you're really lucky, if you commit one of the Deadly Sins of Strategy, you will put yourself in a disadvantaged position ... and likely won't even realize how you got there.

Terrific Plans

*Life is what happens
while you are making other plans*

– John Lennon

Signs when you have lots of plans …
… but have lost sight of what your *real* strategy is

- Everyone can recite the company's goals – but if you ask any individual what the first steps are to translate these goals into reality, most of what you hear is some variant of 'more of same.'

- Management believes that if you set the goals, the strategy will take care of itself. People inside the company agree – and consequently spend their creative energies more on finding ways to make their bonuses (and gain the other goodies of successful job performance) than on making decisions that will strengthen their organization's future position in the market place (see above).

- The company is committed to the strategy planning process, especially when the plans have lots of multicolor graphs and complex charts. Excellence in plan packaging is therefore a skill in high demand and is rewarded accordingly.

- Strategy plans get written annually – and once written, are never looked at again (except for the purpose of updating last year's prose for this year's plan). Meanwhile, and regardless of what the plans or vision statements say, most decisions are driven by meeting short-term financial goals … just as they always have been.

- Statements of the business's approach to the future are full of words about the 'technique du jour' (quality, core competency, customer service, or whatever) without any concrete definition of what these terms mean for *this* business.

- All you have to do is look at what's receiving resources (versus what's being starved) and what's being rewarded (versus what's being punished) and you can immediately tell that the real strategy is radically different from the one management says it is following.

- Whatever the process used, key strategy decisions are based primarily on:

  - what has worked in the past – even though competitive conditions have changed.

  - what was done in the past – even if it didn't work.

  - what some other company did – or what some guru claimed some other company did – even though the circumstances differ substantially.

- If you had to compare business as conducted in the company with a sport, you'd choose crew: eight guys who know how to row but can't see where they are going, being directed by a guy facing forward who can't row … but is still barking orders through his megaphone.

- Employees can't wait until they are fully vested in the corporate stock plan … so they can cash out and put the proceeds elsewhere.

On the first day of my first finance class in business school, the professor entered the room, surveyed the students, and announced that he could summarize all of what we were about to learn in his course. Whereupon he looked into the eyes of the would-be investment bankers, the soon-to-be corporate executives, and – by far the largest group (of which I was part) – the truly clueless, and said: 'Don't run out of cash'.

When you think about playing for success, this prescription is a pretty good place to start. Above and beyond not running out of cash for day-to-day operations, you want to create surpluses, so that after you've paid off what you owe, you can reinvest in your business, reward your employees, and provide returns – or at least credible promises of future returns – to your equity holders. And if you can't create such surpluses, you pretty quickly find yourself lagging further and further behind in your markets, as you become less able to keep up with industry shifts, you can't get the employees you really need, and your cost of capital goes up.

For these reasons, a business managed without some sort of belief about how to win is a business adrift. And, given reasonable alternatives, few people would be willing to invest either wholehearted effort or hard earned cash in such an enterprise – excepting, of course, bottom-fishing investors hoping for a windfall in the event of a hostile takeover. Yet despite the importance of this core belief, many companies confuse prose with strategy, and therefore then assume that words about goals and direction will lead to the desired results.

This confusion is typically exacerbated by two sleights of mind. One is to assume that once the targets have been set – whether in the form of specific financial numbers or broad visionary ambitions – the strategy will take care of itself. Another is to believe that what's said in meetings and written in strategy documents

'I don't like money, actually, but it quiets my nerves.'
– Joe Louis (1914–1981), American prize fighter

'If you would like to know the value of money, go and try to borrow some.'
Benjamin Franklin (1706–1790), American statesman

provides a fair representation of the actual direction being taken. A good number of companies do both: set aggressive aims and put together detailed plans, trusting that a cogent strategy will, some way or the other, arise out of the mix.

Though each of these approaches comes straight from mainstream management thinking, in practice the *real* strategies they create often differ substantially from what management *thinks* it has put into place. Two facts remain: One is that your control of your corporate destiny increases if you know what your real strategy is. The other is that ultimate accountability for a company's real strategy still and always resides at the top of the organization, regardless of the beauty and motivational power of the vision or the stretch goals, or of the elegance and brilliance of the official plans.

Or to put a literary spin on the plaque that Harry S Truman kept on his desk after he became President, Do not ask with whom the buck stops. The buck stops with thee.

Part one
What gets measured gets done ...
... what gets rewarded gets done repeatedly

Imagine the surprise that awaited Peter Harris and Peter Morse, new owners of the famous toy store, FAO Schwartz, when they came across an $11,000 doll house that was sitting in the company's inventory. It was quite an ordinary doll house really, one that you might expect would sell for several hundred dollars. So why was it marked at $11,000? As the new owners later told the story, that answer was that the value of other obsolete inventory, rather than being written off, was being incorporated into the ever-growing price of the doll house. While the write-ups helped managers to meet their financial targets, the practice obviously did nothing to make the company more competitive in its marketplace.

I'd guess that most people reading this book have seen other instances of end-runs around the rules in their own companies – or even participated in one on occasion. The bogus doll house write-up is just a mild variant of what happens everyday everywhere: employees who invent ever more ingenious ways to meet targets, even when the ways they invent are destructive to the business in the long run.

And such deviations are as likely to occur when the targets for which everyone is striving are presented in the form of expansive vision statements as they are when given as straight financial targets. That's because such targets describe primarily the big 'what's': the high-level outcomes that the company seeks to achieve. As long as these desired outcomes are not accompanied by some rough 'how's' – a loose, overall framework within which the outcomes are to be achieved – they will either take on a life of their own (typically when they are linked to strong incentives) or die by neglect (typically when they are not).

The above assertion is, of course, an heretical apostasy in the context of new-age management theory. The au courant idea is that if you create a vision and empower and reward your employees for carrying it out, the employees will create the strategy themselves in a beautiful and organic way. But in one essential respect, managing by vision alone is not substantially different than managing by the numbers alone. In both cases, the strategy does take care of itself, but not necessarily in the ways you might have anticipated. A closer look at managing the what's – but not providing an adequate framework for the how's – provides a perspective on why this is so.

That is the whole problem with being a heretic. One usually must think out everything for oneself.'
– Aubrey Menen (b. 1912), British author

And visions of bonuses danced in their heads: from disk drives to desk tops

Sometimes truth is stranger than fiction, as a number of purchasers of computer components discovered when they unpacked boxes that were supposed to contain hard disks – but instead were filled with bricks. A practical joke? Well, that depends on what you find hilarious. In the actual case, shipping bricks instead of hard drives was just one of a pattern of tactics taken by employees of MiniScribe, a California disk drive manufacturer, to meet the company's goals and thereby earn their bonuses.

According to former customers and employees, other maneuvers included a variety of shady techniques to boost reported revenues (shipping more product to customers than had been ordered and then booking the entire lot as sales before the excess was sent back; counting product shipped to company warehouses as sales rather than inventory) and to reduce reported costs (packaging contaminated disk drives so they could be booked as inventory; tossing other defective drives into a storage area called the 'dog pile' and also booking them – along with the contaminated drives and the returned bricks – as inventory rather than as losses in excess of the reserves for defective merchandise). The result was explosive growth – at least as reported – followed by a crash, entry into bankruptcy proceedings, and subsequent purchase by rival Maxtor at a fire-sale price.

About a decade later, a similar drama unfolded in a highly dissimilar setting: the elementary and secondary school system in the state of Kentucky. Once again, the goal was an ambitious one, and important for the enterprise: to ratchet student performance in basic skills – including reading, writing, and mathematics – to higher standards as measured by comprehensive, essay-based examinations. On the face of it, this is not a radical idea; many countries in Europe and Asia already have such systems in place, and student performance has grown to match the standards. In Kentucky, though, there was a twist: when a school's scores went up, the school received extra funds that could be used for supplemental goodies such as computers and training – or for cash bonuses for teachers. Conversely, when the scores declined, schools got the stick: sanctions, including outside 'experts' who, in extreme cases, became the bosses of the existing school heads and arrived with the power to fire teachers.

The theory was, that between the carrots and the sticks, test scores would rise. And indeed, over half of the state's schools qualified for reward money, almost all of which went to teacher bonuses. But though in many cases the gains were real, in some they were not, as teachers in a variety of schools employed a variety of methods to 'help' their students to perform well on the tests. As subsequently reported in *The Wall Street Journal*, these included passing out the examination questions in advance; allowing students to refer to their textbooks while taking the tests; and editing the essays before they were scored. Being an effective teacher is one of the toughest jobs there is. Add to that new, intense pressures and clear incentives without sufficient time and training to develop the required skills, and sometimes – as at MiniScribe – doing anything to meet the targets will become the strategy.

Though these are extreme cases, they're important because of the number of people involved. In both, the resulting problems weren't due to the actions of one isolated person who stepped way out of bounds (as was alleged in the celebrated 1990s trading scandals at Barings, Sumitomo, and GE's Kidder, Peabody), but to many people taking many inappropriate shortcuts. And therein lies the point: Every organization, regardless of industry, size or scope, has an implicit strategy – that is, an overall pattern of actions taken, resources spent, and rewards given throughout the enterprise. But having an *implicit* strategy is not the same as having a *good* strategy; quite clearly, not all directions are equally attractive. Which leads to the heart of the problem: if you can't see through your beliefs to the

> *'Businesses are nothing more or less than organizations of people trying to get to a jointly defined future.'*
>
> – Howard H. Stevenson, Professor, Harvard Business School

real strategy, you are at risk of thinking you have cracked the code for how to achieve your goals – whatever they may be – when in fact the real strategy being employed may be woefully inadequate, or worse.

Blindside economics: the beguiling beauty of a billion-dollar bogey

How can seemingly legitimate goals – either in the form of financial targets or in the form of visionary ambitions – create an underground strategy that ends you up where you don't want to be? Further digging into the MiniScribe mess turns up some clues. The story starts when Hambrecht and Quist, an investment firm headed by Quentin T. Wiles, took a $20 million position in MiniScribe. A year later, in late 1986, Wiles switched roles, became CEO of the disk drive manufacturer, and had a dream: to build MiniScribe into a billion-dollar company in record time – no mean feat given that the company's revenues had only just hit $185 million that year. His plan for achieving this dream was quite simple – set annual stretch targets, provide a generous bonus plan, and announce the single requirement that to get the dough, you have to hit the goals.

At first, Wiles's approach worked like a charm. Or at least, it certainly seemed to. Starting from the revenue base of $185 million, MiniScribe grew to $362 million the next year, and targeted $660 million for the year after that. Then everything fell apart, starting with an audit that revealed 'massive fraud' and ending with the Maxtor buying the whole operation for short money. Yet according to his friends, Wiles was truly shocked by what the investigators found and believed that he had been 'blindsided' by others within his firm. (For the record, Wiles was subsequently found guilty of three charges of fraud for his part in the debacle.)

Nonetheless, it doesn't appear that the financial targets, though extraordinarily ambitious, would have been impossible to achieve through legitimate means, at least in theory: A competitor, Conner Peripherals, that had only $113 million in sales in 1987, hit over $1.3 billion for fiscal 1990. Nor is measuring and rewarding employees based on stretch targets either new or unduly risky; countless companies have done it and achieved stunning results – just look at GE under Jack Welch. The unacceptable risk comes when, as happened at MiniScribe and a bunch of schools in Kentucky, aggressive targets are set without sufficient overall guidance to help people with the 'how's.'

Guidance on the 'how's' – or what I've called the 'frame' – needn't be complex or exhaustive, but it does need to provide more direction than specific numerical goals or expansive vision statements alone. Consider the approach that Microsoft's Chris Peters took when he was managing the development of Word 6.0 for Windows. According to Julie Bick, who wrote a book about her experiences at Microsoft, this was Peters' description of what he wanted:

Word 6.0 ha[s] to be:
1 *"Auto-Everything" (make everyday tasks such as spelling and formatting automatic)*
2 *A great part of the Office Suite (consistent look and good interaction with Excel and PowerPoint)*
3 *The best upgrade for WordPerfect users (high-quality help and file filters).*

Note that Peters didn't limit his guidance to numerical targets (sell X dollars by Y date) or rely solely on a broad ambition (kill WordPerfect). Nor did he try to solve all the problems for his team. Rather, he described a decision space, the context within which his people could use their creativity to develop a product that would triumph in the marketplace. The overall goals were still ambitious, but he included enough 'how's' to provide a shared framework for action.

The lesson is straightforward: If people's livelihoods and life-styles depend on achieving stretch goals and they aren't given the rough guidelines within which to do so, they will devise their own. This is true if you employ a traditional approach, as Q. T. Wiles did, or if you dress it up in the new business language of 'applying chaos theory to management' or 'leveraging empowered, self-directed work teams in a bottoms-up approach to vision fulfillment.' 'Bricks' come in all sizes, shapes and forms, ranging from the real stuff in MiniScribe's case to a variety of shortcuts and detours that end up sabotaging an organization and its goals.

Ella was right: it don't mean a thing ...
... if it ain't got that swing

'I can't stand to sing the same song the same way two nights in succession. If you can, then it ain't music, it's close order drill, or exercise or yodelling or something, not music.'
– Billie Holliday (1915–1959), American blues great

Jazz great Ella Fitzgerald used to sing 'It don't mean a thing if it ain't got that swing,' promptly punctuating her declaration with a little bit of scat. You won't hear any dispute for her point of view from this quarter, as applied to either be-bop or to business.

Goals – again, whether in the form of financial objectives or visionary statements – only have that swing when they are backed in ways that feel real to the participants. The most tangible way of providing swing is, of course, to provide financial incentives, as Q.T. Wiles and the state of Kentucky both did. But ideas can also provide tremendous motivational power. The key questions are, do the people inside the company see the high-flying ideas as feasible on the one hand – and the promised incentives as desirable on the other.

These are tougher questions than may at first appear. I am constantly surprised at the number of companies where the goals, the incentives, or both seem real to the CEO who is promulgating them, but have become little more than corporate elevator music to everyone else in the organization. In these cases, there's no need for a loose musical score that motivates everyone to play roughly the same tune without strict supervision; who cares about the 'how's' when no one believes in the 'what'?

In the worst cases, the goals slip from the extraordinary to the extraterrestrial; they sound great to the people who promulgate them but come across as completely deranged to everyone else. The disconnect typically occurs with executives who have read too many books on visionary management but have neglected to determine whether it is even remotely possible for *their* companies to gain access to the skills and resources required to turn these dreams into reality. At Komatsu, perhaps the most famous example of visionary strategy, management used an extraordinary goal – 'Maru-C' ('encircle Caterpillar' in English) – to propel this earth-moving equipment company from weak domestic player to worldwide force. But here's the key: At every step in the process, Komatsu management also provided a clear game plan for building the next level of organizational skills, thereby keeping an extraordinary goal tethered to reality. (The 10-second version of the story – Komatsu started by increasing its investment in R&D, committing to a quality-improvement process, and moving stepwise through a set of specific targets: first improve the quality of the small and medium size bulldozers; then reduce the costs of these 'dozers; next improve the quality of the export product – the large earth-moving machines; then reducing these costs of the big machines; and so on.) Though the overall goal may have sounded almost delusional, the individual steps were within the realm of imagination – at least for people with ambition and the willingness to put their efforts where their hopes were.

Komatsu, though, is the exception rather than the rule. More typically, people see the goals as achievable in theory but not in practice. Or they understand what needs to be done but don't believe that they will either be permitted to take the required actions or helped in their efforts to achieve them. In both situations, top managers are often confident that everyone in the company – and certainly their senior managers – understand the goals they've set. After all, they say, look at how many times I said this in my speeches, memos and reports. And further research usually shows that they are correct, at least in one respect: just about everyone who is supposed to can parrot back whatever it is that their bosses have been preaching.

And there the transmission stops; message duly received, recorded, and promptly discarded as irrelevant.

Is this happening in your organization? A telling question is to ask what the first steps are for translating the 'new' goals into reality. If the answers you get are variants of doing what has always been done (though perhaps more frantically), or if you get only blank stares in response, that's a pretty good sign of less substance than meets the eye. Ditto if you receive cogent, thoughtful answers, followed by an explanation that these steps won't be taken because attempting to do so has low odds for being rewarded – and very high odds for getting punished. The result, more often than not, is more of the same, as people resign themselves to doing their jobs pretty much as they always have.

And even when both the what's and the how's are reasonable, sometimes neither the tangible nor intangible rewards are sufficient to lead to the desired changes in behavior. The usual cause of the lapse is the assumption that doing what's right for the company should be motivation enough for the employees. We'll take a closer look at this in Chapters 4 and 5, stopping here only to note the cautionary tale of the US company that tried to use a 'Rude Hog' contest to discourage its service representatives from being surly with customers. An obvious and desirable goal, right? And certainly the contest rules were simple enough; the rep with the lowest customer satisfaction ratings for the period got tagged with the label. The hitch was that many of the employees didn't see why they should bother to care about customers – much less make an effort to be nice. But they did think that it would be highly entertaining to compete for new lows in the ratings, which they promptly did. Rather than being an incentive for providing better service, receiving the Rude Hog designation became a badge of honor.

So the theory is right; aggressive goals tightly linked to attractive incentives will create purposeful and coordinated action. But when such goals are set in the absence of some rough, overall framework, the actions they produce can backfire. Take away the incentives, and the odds of a backfire go down, but so do the odds of purposeful and coordinated action. In either case, managing by numbers or visions alone can lead to the illusion that you know what your real strategy is, when in fact your company is operating on cruise control.

Part two
What gets written makes a plan …
… what gets *done* makes a strategy

The buzz on strategy has something of a pogo-stick feel to it. Plans crammed with data and charts are the thing, some argue; no, say others, planning is *passé*, made irrelevant by the far greater efficacy of visionary ambitions and financial targets. Then in the midst of all the hoopla, strategic planning comes back into style; even *Business Week* runs a cover story on its 'sudden' return. And once again, people in companies around the world begin believing that if you write a strategy down, it must be good – especially if you have included lots of charts and spreadsheets and other evidence of extensive analysis.

Although the label may have mutated (from 'strategic plan' to 'business plan', 'market plan', 'strategic review' and the like), in actual fact, strategic planning never died in the first instance. And for good reason. The essence of any strategy is where the resources are being allocated. Show me where the cash is going, and I can show you the bones of the real strategy. A planning process provides a time-out for an organization to reconsider its bets: where it has been allocating its resources, where it should allocate them in the future, and why.

'Where is the wisdom we have lost in knowledge? Where is the knowledge we have lost in information?'
– T.S. Eliot (1888–1965), American or British (depending on your perspective) poet

This is not to say that plans require the kind of copious documentation in which many companies indulged in the 1970s and 1980s. Even today, if you walk into many corporate offices, you're likely to find bookshelves straining under the weight of reports, studies, memoranda, charts and spreadsheets – all of which have been buffed and polished and look absolutely terrific. But in many cases, the formal strategies embodied in these reams of papers and collection of disks describe paths of action that are quite different from the actual strategies being created.

When the actual strategy leads to success in the market place, this divergence of the real from the written is less of a problem, although it does indicate that the company doesn't have a *conscious* understanding of what it is doing right. In many cases, however, the divergence has just the opposite result: the company experiences losses in market share or profit margin – or disregards early warning signs that such losses are about to occur – and doesn't understand how its own actions created these results.

In these cases, misreading the real strategy is highly dangerous to the future health of the enterprise. In some instances, the disconnect is due to pure fantasy: the plans represent what management *wishes* the company to become, quite apart from the real actions to be taken. In many others, it's due to incorrect notions of what it takes to build a framework for strategic thinking. And one of the most pervasive, and dangerous, of these incorrect notions is the idea of 'sustainable competitive advantage.'

Of fortresses built on shifting sands: the mirage of sustainability

Read most strategy plans – and most budgets – and you'll find the assumption, implicit in both the text and the numbers, that what provides advantage to the company today will provide similar advantages to the company tomorrow. This should not be a surprise. It's easier to put together plans and budgets if you keep the same things constant, including the basis for how you mean to succeed in the market. Plus there's the comfort of the familiar. And then there's the fact that for years, both academic and practical definitions of strategy has been rooted in the idea of 'sustainable competitive advantage.'

Today that idea is under sharp attack. The spark for the dispute was lit, I believe, by the 1982 book, *In Search of Excellence*.

Here is what happened. In the wake of *In Search of Excellence*'s multi-million book sales, many people began to wonder about what had happened to the 'excellent companies' that Peters and Waterman had chronicled. Michele Clayman was one of these people. So she took the same six criteria of performance (three measuring growth and three measuring financial returns) that Peters and Waterman used to delineate their sample of excellent companies, and applied them to the 29 excellent companies that were still publicly traded in 1985. When she compared the performance of these 29 companies over two time periods, 1981–1985 (post-pub) versus 1976–1980 (pre-pub), she made the following discoveries:

- The rate of asset growth declined in 25 of the 29 companies.
- The rate of equity growth declined in 27 of the 29.
- The market-to-book ratios declined in 20 of the 29.
- The average return on total capital declined in 24 of the 29.
- The average return on equity declined in 23 of the 29.
- The average returns on sales declined in 24 of the 29.

Clayman also identified the 39 *worst* companies in 1980, based on the same criteria for the 1976–1980 period. When she looked at these companies for the second time period, she found that the former losers outperformed the excellent companies on the six criteria by a significant margin – and beat the S&P 500 by 12 percent per year, versus 1 percent for the excellent companies.

Clayman explained her results in terms of a 'regression to the mean' – the statistical tendency of the performance of both leaders and laggards to moderate over time and approach the average for the group. But I think a more useful explanation lies in the dynamics of advantage. After all, competitors and would-be competitors are always seeking success, just as you are. If they can, they will take or create opportunities to share in advantages that you already possess.

That's how Wilkinson Sword Group Ltd. got into the razor-blade business when, several decades ago, Gillette invented a new stainless steel blade, but chose not to introduce it. Gillette evidently figured that superior blades meant more shaves per blade, and that more shaves per blade meant lower unit sales. But not wanting to let the technology go to waste, Gillette decided to sell it to Wilkinson, who posed no threat in the shaving category. Wilkinson, in turn, wanted the technology because the British company, perhaps in keeping with the Biblical admonition about beating swords into ploughshares, was expanding into the garden-tool business. Though neither entity saw the other as a potential competitor, Wilkinson did produce a limited quantity of razor blades as a promotion for its new garden tools. And that in turn led to the startling discovery that people would do almost anything to get their hands on the blades. Eventually Wilkinson recognized the opportunity and moved to capitalize on it with Wilkinson Sword Blades, and Gillette had a new competitor. (Note that Wilkinson's move into the shaving business was not the beginning of the end for Gillette. Like all good category leaders,

Gillette abhors the idea of reverting to the mean and has kept renewing and recreating its advantages, thereby continuing to strengthen its already strong position after Wilkinson's inadvertent entry.)

Despite Wilkinson's good fortune, though, it's relatively rare for one company to be able to purchase another's competitive advantage almost by accident, as happened in this case. Rather, when competitors and would-be competitors set about to find ways to share in or co-opt your advantage, they do so consciously, looking to invent around patents, change regulations, or crash your exclusive relationships. And if they can't share in your advantage, you can be sure that they are always working hard to create new ways to succeed and, in the process, to make your advantages irrelevant or, worse, to convert them into liabilities (which, surely, was the lesson the Red Coats learned at the hands of the scrappy Massachusetts Minute Men in 1776).

'HERE the men of Boston proved themselves independent courageous freemen worthy to raise issues that were to concern the liberty and happiness of millions yet unborn.'
– sign at entrance of the Old South Meeting House, Boston, Massachusetts

Alexander Randall, an entrepreneur who founded the Boston Computer Exchange (and has since moved on to less taxing endeavors in the Virgin Islands), compares this process to stopping an enemy convoy of armored tanks. Attacking a tank from the front is hopeless – the armored plate is too strong. The same is true for the side or back. But tanks are gas guzzlers; they get gallons to the mile rather than miles to the gallon. If you can attack the gas trucks, you can stop the tanks.

The battle of the bottles ...
... and other fights to immobilize the gas trucks

Because competitors are always devising techniques for immobilizing their opponents' tanks, plans based on the assumption of sustainable advantages often give a false sense of security. The classics are well known: Canon's invention of a disposable cartridge turned Xerox's awesome after-sales support network into a fixed-cost liability for the small-copier segment of the market; Toyota's development of a fast-changeover production process allowed the company to offer more models with minimal stocks of each, thereby turning General Motors' huge economies of scale from long product runs into an inventory-cost nightmare; a college student's premise that personal computers could be sold by mail transformed the competitive landscape first in the US and then in Europe, as Dell Computer made the retail distribution advantage of companies like Compaq and IBM into an irrelevant and costly extra for a large set of buyers.

Less well known is the Swiss watch maker story. No, not the one about quartz mechanisms and the Japanese. The story I'm referring to starts earlier, in the 1950s in the United States, when the Swiss makers had effectively locked up jewelry stores, at the time the dominant retail channel for watches. Then the United States Time Company moved into nontraditional channels – drug stores and other low-end outlets – forcing the Swiss into a strategic corner. Not following Timex would cut their access to a huge, growing customer base. But following Timex would jeopardize the jewelers' loyalty and cooperation, demean the image of Swiss watches, and add to Timex's legitimacy. Not willing to incur these losses, the Swiss were effectively frozen out of the new game that Timex had created.

Or consider the cola wars between Coke and Pepsi. In 1916, Coca-Cola introduced the swirled 6½ ounce bottle that became its signature. Distinctive and perfectly designed to fit the hand, Coke trademarked the bottle and used it in its ad. In the late 1930s, Pepsi, then a very small rival, decided to attack the icon in the US by introducing a 12-ounce bottle for the same price as Coke's 6½ ounce package. In 1939, this radio jingle hit the air:

Pepsi Cola hits the spot,
Twelve full ounces, that's a lot.
Twice as much for a nickel, too.
Pepsi Cola is the drink for you.

What could Coke do? Cutting price was difficult because of all the five-cent soda machines around. A larger bottle also wasn't feasible – the same shape at twice the size would have fit only the biggest hands. And the company's bottlers had a billion or so of the 6½ ounce bottles in inventory. The result was that Coke kept its famous trademark bottle and Pepsi grew in the American retail market.

Several decades later, in the early 1970s, Pepsi returned to a similar strategy. Despite Pepsi's previous success in competing through packaging, the company recognized that 'The Bottle' was still one of Coke's most fearsome advantages in US grocery stores, and instructed a new employee, John Sculley, to come up with a competitive bottle design. As part of this task, Sculley undertook an extended, in-home product test with 350 families. But about eight or nine weeks into the test, Sculley noticed that the more gallons of soft drinks on hand, the more each family drank, an effect caused by the research but not what the research had been designed to test.

After a look at the tests, Sculley decided that he had been trying to solve the wrong problem. 'The research told us that if you could get in the door, there were few limits to [Pepsi] consumption,' he concluded. 'Instead of redesigning the standard bottle, it became obvious that … we should launch new, larger, and more varied packaging.' The company did, and within four years, Pepsi passed Coke in share of the market for bottled soft drink sales in the US, as measured by Nielsen market-tracking data. Three years after that, Coke suspended use of its signature bottle, once one of its greatest assets. (Coke subsequently brought back a variant of its famous swirl bottle. The Coke exec in charge of the revival was Sergio Zyman, who had worked for Sculley at Pepsi in the 1970s.)

Certainly some things have changed since the first cola war of 1939. The velocity of competitive moves tends to be faster, and the geographic scope broader. But the general principal remains: advantages shift. Your odds of winning increase dramatically if you understand your current advantages and are clear about the assumptions you are making about how to maintain a competitive edge, even as the specific advantages themselves change.

'Life is the art of drawing suffi-cient conclusions from insufficient data.'

– Samuel Butler (1835–1902), British author

This isn't to say that all advantages are equally ephemeral; some last longer than others. Louisiana-based McIlhenny Co. invented Tabasco sauce at about the time of the American Civil War. One hundred and thirty years later, the company had never changed its recipe, still picked the peppers used in its sauce by hand, and only in the late 1980s introduced other Tabasco products (including 'Tabasco 7-Spice Chili Recipe'). Said Paul McIlhenny, one of the approximately ninety family shareholders in the company in 1990: 'We've gotten more aggressive than previously, and I think the next hundred years will see us trying even more new things.' Good thing. Salsas and other peppers-based condiments have since become one of the hottest food categories in the US, and new competitors seem to enter the market almost monthly.

Nevertheless, the McIlhenny Companies of the world are few and far between. For the rest of us, the lesson is plain: advantages need to be maintained, renewed and recreated, because somewhere, someplace, a would-be competitor is taking aim at yours. For this reason, it's better to be agile than strong, as long as you know what your targets are and why you want to achieve them.

Part three
Earth-bound business:
retrieving strategy from the stratosphere

But what of value is left in the average strategic plan if you delete all the implicit assumptions about sustainable advantages? In many cases, not much. Oh, there's plenty more stuff, all right. But the words, data and analyses are often irrelevant to the decisions being made, by virtue of being either perfectly useless or merely practically useless.

Economist and columnist Thomas Sowell tells a story that exemplifies the first category. It seems that Sowell was introduced to the head of the economic forecasting unit of a large corporation who promptly informed his visitor that his company had thirty years' worth of comprehensive economic data. Sowell allowed as this was a good thing, as it meant that the company's forecasting guru presumably could use these data to do actual-versus-forecast analyses of the predictions the company had made over past thirty years. The remark was met with palpable silence. Then the guru announced his assessment: 'I can see,' he said, 'that we are not going to get along.'

But it's the practically useless material that dominates in most strategic plans; that is, analysis and data that reflect the mainstream management literature, are academically correct, and remain largely untethered to the real-life decisions. Thus one sees elaborate analyses of industry structure or core competencies, disconnected to a point of view about the actions to be taken – or to a plan for executing those actions that is even remotely feasible. Or one sees *au courant* words such as quality, empowerment, productivity, low-cost producer, customer-driven; all of which are used in the absence of concrete definition of meaning for *this* organization, and all of which therefore have devolved into corporate-speak; fine sounding, but essentially content-free.

The 'good deals at a profit over time' standard ...
... and four acid tests to see if you are meeting it

Readers of *Fad Surfing in the Boardroom* will not be shocked at this assessment of fancy words with little meaning. I wrote that book to poke fun at what I called 'bizbuz' and then to get people to think about how to put the various management terms and tools to work for their organizations, rather than to be worked over by them. I abbreviate the framework I used in that book to navigate through the fads as the 'good deal at profit over time' standard. That's my shorthand for what companies have to do to build surpluses: provide a better deal to their target customers than their competitors do while still making a profit and continuing to do so over time as the environment changes. And that's the foundation I use in this book to explore and explode the core beliefs of what organizations need to do to have an economic model that makes sense, employees who are effective in their jobs, and information that can aid in achieving the outcomes being sought.

Bizbuz:
A good way to sound smart while preventing any leakage of content into a conversation.

The danger of the first three deadly sins concerns the first of these, the soundness of the economic model that underlies a company's strategy. A look at the economic model inherent in many budgets, pro formas, and strategic plans shows why. That's because the typical model used in these settings consists of taking the price realized in the market, multiplying it times unit sales, and then subtracting out the pertinent fixed and variable costs to reach the bottom line. Simple, right? But though simple, it lacks one critical variable that drives the prices you can realize, the costs you incur, and the volume you can gain in the market. And that variable is the benefits customers receive. For this reason, when I picture the generic economic model, I think of the price-to-cost relationship as the right side of a triangle, anchored on the left corner by benefits to the customer. The picture I get from this addition, combined with four acid tests as described on the next page, is shown in Fig. 1.1.

Though this triangle is also pretty simple, I find it useful as a

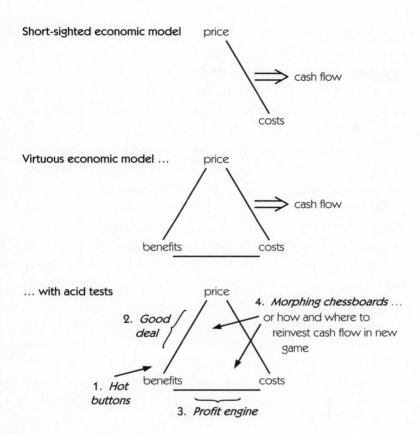

Fig. 1.1 Good-deal triangle.

way to highlight four major bets that, while implicit in every strategy, aren't always evident. The first of these is what benefits your need to offer; the second, what benefits-to-price profile makes your product a better deal to the target market than what your competitors provide; the third, what benefits-to-*costs* profile allows you to offer this deal and still make adequate margins; and finally, fourth, what reinvestments you need to make in order to maintain your good-deal-at-a-profit position in the future. To delve into these four bets further, I've developed four 'acid tests.' The tests build on each other, so you need to be able to pass all four without changing assumptions midstream. (Don't laugh; I've seen plenty of bright executives do exactly that.)

These are the four:

1. **The 'hot buttons' test.** This test focuses on the benefits corner of the good-deal triangle. To answer it, you have know your target customers' hot buttons; that is, what your customers and potential customers care about more and what they care about less. The question you need to answer is this: 'Does your product or service score enough points from enough customers to make a potential market?'

   (In a surprising number of cases, company assumptions about the decision weights used by customers are quite off the mark. Swimsuits provide a great example, as demonstrated by research conducted in the US in 1987 by the Swimsuit Manufacturers Association, better known as SWIM. The research showed that sexy suits didn't look good on most prospective customers, and that in turn meant, as a supplier to the industry delicately put it, 'that most women would rather have a root canal without Novocain than buy a swimsuit.' In the rush to make hot suits for hot babes, the industry had forgotten about what one would have thought was an obvious hot button for the rest of their slightly-to-profoundly out-of-shape market – beachwear that, if not flattering, was at least not totally inappropriate or grossly embarrassing.)

2. **The 'good deal' test.** For this test, price and competitors are added to the mix. To pass it, you have to be clear about the benefits of your product at your prices, the benefits of substitutes and competitors' products at their prices, and how much time and money your customers have to spend in making their purchase decisions. The double question to be answered here is: first, 'how much of your potential market evaluates your product's benefits-to-price profile as the best deal given their requirements?' and second, 'is this portion of the market sufficient to support the business you want to build?'

(It may be obvious, but still worth pointing out, that even great products can be sunk by poor pricing, which is what happened to the Philips CD-i compact-disk interactive player. Though the CD-i had been a success in Europe, it flopped in America, with cumulative five-year sales from its 1991 introduction reaching only 400,000 units. A big part of the problem: initially priced at $799, the player couldn't compete with the far less capable, but also far less expensive game systems from Sega and Nintendo. A better approach might have been to have priced the system at $399, as suggested by Philips' American team, with the intent of making the money on the software.)

3. **The 'profit engine' test.** The good-deal test indicates how much cash is likely to come in; this test focuses on how much of that cash will stick to the business. Now the issue is whether your benefits-to-*cost* position will allow you to meet the market requirements and still generate enough cash for reinvestment in the business and meeting other goals (unless, of course, you generate such a good story about future earnings that the capital markets shower you with dough). The component questions for this test require you to have some understanding of your benefits-to-cost position relative to the benefits-to-cost positions of both direct competitors and substitutes. Here's the test: 'Will your benefits-to-cost position allow you to amass enough cash to meet your organization's goals, including reinvestment targets, while continuing to provide a good deal for your target customers?'

(Keeping the benefits in focus when calculating costs isn't always top of mind when executives are making decisions about which costs to add and which to cut. This may be why Procter & Gamble was so

---

'Remember history, "the Boston Tea Party," where the English wanted to tax our tea? The colonials decided to give them a wake-up call, and it worked. We, too, can give the "Big Guys" a wake-up call. Let dust collect on Procter & Gamble products.'
– letter from Katherina Roberts, to the editor of *The Oneida Dispatch,* Oneida, New York

---

surprised when it announced that it was terminating its coupon programs in three New York cities, with the expectation of lower prices for customers – and ended up with customer boycotts, legislative hearings, and the threat of an anti-trust probe by the New York state Attorney General's office. P&G saw the move as one that would save money for both the company and its customers, while relieving customers of the 'inconvenience' of dealing with coupons. But though P&G saw the coupons as an unnecessary cost, customers regarded them as not only providing direct savings, but also the thrill of the chase – an emotional benefit, but one with very high salience to a segment of very noisy and ultimately very powerful customers.)

4. **The 'morphing chessboard' test.** People take different perspective on change. Your preferred approach may be based on revolutionary moves or evolutionary ones; you might like to strike first and act preemptively or to adapt quickly and cleverly to actions taken by others. But no matter how you like to proceed, you still have to invest some of the cash you amass today into creating future positions on the first three tests – the hot buttons you intend to hit, the deals you plan to offer, and the profit engines you mean to run.

    And that's the point of the morphing-chessboard test which, though listed last, is really a go-along question for the others. Its focus is on who could: change position and how in the game as played by current rules; create new spaces that no one else yet sees; or change the rules themselves. This requires imagination – about what you and current competitors could do, who else could enter the current game space, how customer needs and wants might shift, what kinds of sneak attacks would be particularly effective or worrisome depending on your point of view, and how fast you need to be able to act. The concluding questions here are: 'What you are doing today that will allow you to change the game preemptively or react to change by others quickly and effectively enough that you gain from your moves?'

(Note the modifier of 'quickly and effectively enough.' Then remember that Microsoft was not first into the Internet game. And that when it did enter, it moved quickly enough and effectively enough to cause major headaches for earlier entrants who initially appeared to have captured the 'first-mover' advantage.)

These four acid tests don't replace the tools of strategic analysis. Structural analysis, for example, is still important as a barometer of industry attractiveness and potential industry evolution. What they can do, however, is to help you identify and then challenge the implicit beliefs that underlie your visions, goals, and plans. You may not like what you see – as explored further in the next two chapters – but making your beliefs explicit is the first step to making more realistic predictions, and thereby gaining higher odds on achieving the outcomes you seek.

• • •

Imagine my surprise on the extremely humid and exceptionally hot day in Manhattan when I hailed a cab and Akmed B stopped to pick me up. Here's why I was astonished. The air conditioning had been running, so the car was delightfully cool. The car was also spotlessly clean as was Akmed, who was well groomed and dressed in a polo shirt and long trousers. An added treat: Akmed was friendly and polite without being intrusive.

If you've ever been in New York city, you'll immediately understand the source of my amazement. And if you haven't, then what you need to know is that the standards of cleanliness in most cabs and for most cabbies are usually quite a bit lower than you might have preferred, especially on a really hot day. Worse, when you ask for the air conditioning to be turned on, you'll either get grudging acquiescence or, as likely, be told that the system is 'broken.'

After awhile, Akmed and I got to talking, and I asked him why he chose to conduct his business so differently than other cabbies typically do. 'Well,' he said, 'other guys don't want to run their air conditioners because it costs them more in gas. I figure it costs me about $7 to $11 a day more to keep the car cool. But then I get more tips, not from everybody, but from enough people to make about $25 to $50 more per day, easy, than those guys do.' He also told me that he showered before each shift, and made sure that he was wearing clean clothes. 'You know,' he confided, 'a lot of other guys don't do that, and the customers, they don't like it.' Amen. I gave Akmed a huge tip.

Akmed succeeds because he has intuitively figured out the answers to the acid tests. You may think that the answers to these tests should be obvious. But if they are, why haven't the other cab drivers figured them out – especially as economic theory would tell us that people whose income is composed almost entirely by tips, such as New York cabbies, would develop implicit strategies that could pass the acid tests and thereby improve their incomes? But in fact, in cabs in Manhattan (not to mention restaurants just about everywhere), the opposite pertains most of the time.

Why?

And how do you know that the same isn't happening in your organization as well?

Sin #2

Outstanding Products

*There is no reason anyone would want
a computer in their home.*

– Ken Olsen
Founder, Digital Equipment Company
and CEO at the time of the PC revolution

Signs when you're certain your products are outstanding ...
... but the market is moving elsewhere

- Competitors are offering new products that everyone inside your company insists are losers (but that customers are buying in increasing quantities).

- You have developed a long list of adjectives to describe target customers who buy competitors' products, which starts with 'irrational' and 'not very smart' and then goes on from there.

- Company executives talk about what customers 'should' want and why they 'should' like it – and become agitated or irritated (or both) when the customers don't behave as expected (see item above).

- The company conducts little if any research of basic product concepts, because:

  ◦ test results that showed anything other than the internal view would be entirely too inconvenient to be considered

  ◦ the only question ever asked internally about basic product concepts is 'why waste money to test what we already know to be true'?

- Other market research on the company's products is highly efficient, as it focuses almost exclusively on those select attributes that insiders have previously agreed are the most important to customers – regardless of market clues to the contrary. The Market Research department complies; after all, its mission is to produce findings that make its internal customers feel smart – and that thereby allow these insiders to continue to operate within their collective comfort zone.

- No one can really explain, using real data, the relative importance customers assign to each of the components that make up the products being sold; therefore, all benefits are considered of equal weight, or the CEO's preferences are used as a proxy for the customers' preferences.

- Market anomalies are routinely ignored. Asking 'why' these anomalies have occurred is considered evidence of either an idle mind or, worse, of a trouble maker in the ranks.

- The people who talk about being 'close to the customer' are, of course, certain that they already are.

Whatever hen John R. Boyd served as a US Air Force fighter pilot during the Korean War, he puzzled over a military mystery. Why was it that the American F-86s were wiping the floor with the Soviet-made MIG-15s, when by all current military logic, it was the MIGs that should have been winning the battles? After all, the MIGs could climb faster and higher than the F-86s and were generally considered by the US military brass to be the superior fighter plane, yet it was the F-86s that dominated the skies over the 38th parallel. Boyd's conclusion, after a first-hand review of the data: the F-86s had better visibility and a faster roll rate, and the USAF pilots could therefore change course more quickly than the MIG-15s. In the heavens above Korea, agility was better than flat-out speed.

'That is the whole secret of successful fighting. Get your enemy at a disadvantage; and never, on any account, fight him on equal terms.'
– Arms and the Man, George Bernard Shaw (1856–1950)

Over the rest of his Air Force career, Boyd built on this analysis and, in the process, transformed US air battle strategy and fighter plane design. But though Boyd focused on military applications, his insight about the F-86 is also significant for business, in at least two respects. For one thing, it's a great illustration of how easy it is for smart people to see their own products incorrectly. In this case, Boyd revolutionized US air military strategy by reframing the definition of the F-86, and he reframed the definition of the F-86 simply by looking at the plane through the eyes of its ultimate consumers – the pilots themselves. Then, some years later, when Boyd participated in designing the F-16, the successor to the F-15, he used the same logic to ditch some of the higher tech bells and whistles, in exchange for yet more agility – and a purchase price about half that of the F–15.

On another level, Boyd's conclusion about the real benefits of the F-86 provides a great metaphor for the virtues of agility in business strategy in general – and in dealing with customer hot buttons in particular; sharp visibility to spot when shifts are occurring or could be induced to occur, and a fast roll rate to respond to these changes in a timely way. Boyd himself took a similar line of thinking on the military front and expanded his analysis of the F-86s versus the MIG-15s into what he called 'the OODA

Loop' – observation, orientation, decision, and action – as the basis of air-attack strategy.

Many readers will recognize the OODA Loop as a kissing cousin to the PDCA cycle (plan, do, check, act) that characterizes the approach taken in many Total Quality methodologies. I like Boyd's version better, especially since it puts observation before planning, as shown in Fig. 2–1. Yet accurate observation is tough when you're already certain that you understand your product exactly as your customers do. Then, seeing only what you expect to see, you risk missing important clues about how your target customers' hot buttons are shifting over time, a problem often exacerbated by poorly designed market research that provides false (but reassuring) confirmations of internal beliefs. All of this is why I like to start the 'observation' step of the 'business-OODA Loop' with the benefits corner of the good-deal triangle. For while what a company sells is at the heart of its strategy, it's remarkably easy to offer a set of benefits that customers don't value highly – and to miss some that they do.

'Nothing is easier than self-deceit. For what each man wishes, that he also believes to be true.'
– Desmosthenes (c. 384–322 BC)

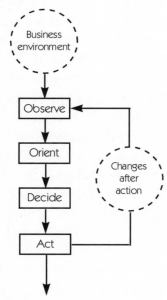

Fig. 2.1 Business OODA Loop.

Part one
There's no button like a hot button
(unless it's your own)

Products are like children – if they're yours, it's hard to see why everyone else doesn't perceive the same beauty, elegance and genius that you do. This is understandable, since running a business requires a belief that you're providing a set of products or services that your market views as a reasonable deal – otherwise, why would you presume that your enterprise has a shot of staying afloat? Yet in a surprising number of cases, not only do the sellers misperceive what the customers want or could want, they don't even really understand the basic concept of their product as their customers define it. A classic example is the microwave oven.

Misreading the customer:
the microwave oven wars

Profile of an opportunity lost

The product:	The microwave oven
The inventor:	Raytheon Company, which introduced the first microwave oven in 1947, a year after Raytheon researcher Percy Spencer filed the patent on the basic technology used in microwave cooking
The venue:	USA
The prize:	440,000 units in 1973; 12,400,000 in 1986; 7,700,000 in 1996
The initial leaders:	Litton Microwave Cooking Products Division and the Amana subsidiary of Raytheon's Major Appliances Group, with a combined market share of 75% in 1973

The concept:	A new technology that would replace the kitchen oven and, to some extent, the stovetop, by making cooking faster and more energy-efficient
The reality:	A device that, in the customers' eyes, was great for heating up and defrosting, and miserable for roasting meats or baking bread
The strategy:	Despite growing evidence to the contrary, stick with the concept of the microwave oven as a total kitchen device – complete with browning units and automatic cooking codes – rather than thinking about it as a smaller, special-purpose cooking appliance
The result:	By 1986, a slew of new entrants led by Japanese and Korean manufacturers had swallowed the $3 billion market by focusing primarily on small, simple units – leaving the former leaders with a mere 12% share. Two years later, Litton exited the business; eight years after that, Amana's share had declined to just 2% of the market that it and Litton had once owned.

The story of how Litton and Amana got left behind in the microwave oven wars is in part the story of two companies that invested disproportionately in products that ultimately didn't match the needs of the very market they created. Since most managers think their products or services are a terrific match for what their customers want, one might be tempted to dismiss this example as an anomaly, or as the kind of trap that present-day managers are certainly clever enough to avoid. But in fact, understanding why customers do what they do and how they therefore evaluate the 'benefits' corner of the good-deal triangle is one of the trickiest tasks in business, regardless of how seasoned or intelligent the company's leadership may be.

'Approachin' at the right side':
the product genius of George Washington Plunkitt

The need to understand customer hot buttons is an old idea, of course, and doesn't necessarily require advanced statistical methods. Consider the approach taken by New Yorker George Washington Plunkitt, a Tamany Hall political underboss of the 1880s, as he explained his hold on the voters in his district:

> ... *you must study human nature and act accordin'. You can't study human nature in books. Books is a hindrance more than anything else ... To learn real human nature you have to go among the people ... I know every man, woman and child in the Fifteenth District ... I know what they like and what they don't like, what they are strong at and what they are weak in, and I reach them by approachin' at the right side ... I don't trouble them with political arguments. I just study human nature and act accordin'.*

'My choice early in life was either to be a piano-player in a whorehouse or a politician. And to tell the truth there's hardly any difference.'
– Harry S Truman (1884–1972), 33rd President of the United States

For companies, though, locating the 'right side' requires figuring out the implicit rating scales that customers use to evaluate all the components of the many products available to them. Some of these components are clearly visible; they're the tangible elements of appearance, performance and packaging – things that can be easily described and measured. And then there are the intangibles – how the product is displayed, sold, delivered, and serviced; its image and reputation; the promises inherent in its brand name; and so on. With so many potential sources of product value, it's no wonder that uncovering customers' hot buttons and determining which ones are most important in the purchase decision can be so difficult. Which brings us back to microwave ovens.

Necessity is not the mother of invention; invention is the mother of necessity

The microwave oven story really starts in 1946 when Percy Spencer, a Raytheon scientist working on radar applications, stood near a magnetron, a device that generates microwaves, and noticed that a chocolate bar in his pocket had melted. Though one shudders to think what else might have been affected, this accidental discovery launched a new industry, though not initially in the US. The reason: No one in the 1950s could imagine a need for microwave ovens in American homes.

The opportunity was clearer in Japan, where small kitchens without Western-style ovens made the new invention more attractive. Even so, the few US manufacturers who recognized an export opportunity didn't pursue it, believing that the expected returns would not justify the required effort. In consequence, while the technology was 'made in the USA.,' it was sold to the Japanese who developed it further, built a large market at home, and later entered the US market with considerable product experience. The Japanese manufacturers also had substantially lower costs due to their cumulative manufacturing volume, particularly for the magnetron. As might have been predicted, both the product experience and the cost structure proved critical in the world-wide battle for market share.

Given the nature of life in the early 1950s, one could easily understand why the US companies neither anticipated a giant domestic market for microwave ovens, nor appreciated how letting go of the core technology would influence their future position in that market. After all, the need for preparing food at warp speed at home – or in the office, dorm room, or any other place microwave ovens now reside – was hardly evident during the Eisenhower years. Relatively few women worked outside the home, students who lived at colleges ate in school cafeterias, and – though this is now hard to remember – popcorn was made with oil, in a pot, on top of the stove.

The inability to anticipate the requirements of a future market when no immediate needs exist is not unique to the microwave oven industry. Microsoft's aggressive pursuit of the Internet had a late start, in part due to Bill Gates' initial skepticism about whether there really was any money to be made in this market – or as Gates himself said in his May 1995 memo, 'The Internet Tidal Wave': 'I have gone through several stages of increasing my view of its importance. Now I assign the Internet the highest level.'

In fact, myopia about new markets is a constant in business. Here are a few of the classics:

'I don't know what it is. I don't want to know what it is. My customers are screaming about it. Make the pain go away.'
– what J. Allard remembers Steve Ballmer, Executive Vice President of Microsoft, telling him about the Internet, around 1993

- In 1876, Western Union refused the opportunity to buy, for $100,000, all of Alexander Graham Bell's patents on the telephone, an invention the company dismissed as 'an electrical toy.'

- In 1897, the president of Remington Arms turned down the opportunity to buy the patent on the typewriter because, as its president said, 'No mere machine can replace a reliable and honest clerk.'

- In 1927, Harry M. Warner, head of Warner Brothers, initially dismissed the idea of motion pictures with sound. His view on the idea was simple: 'Who the hell wants to hear actors talk?'

- In the last quarter of the twentieth century, the following companies made these decisions about participating in the Internet market space:
   - IBM turned down the opportunity to build the network
   - Control Data, developer of one of the world's first super computers, did too
   - AT&T, once the Net was up, declined the chance to run it as a monopoly service
   - The US Postal Service took a pass when offered first dibs on an e-mail system.

In all these cases, as with the US microwave oven market in the 1950s, what turned out to be the future looked preposterous, or irrelevant – or both – at inception.

Technologies create markets ...
... and markets modify technologies

Even after US companies became interested in microwave cooking for the home consumer and skillfully created the domestic market, another problem occurred: The consumers shifted their definition of what a microwave oven should be well before the pioneers shifted theirs.

This shift in consumers' perception of the product and how it could fill their needs occurred slowly, making it even more difficult to detect. In the early phase of the market's development, producers and consumers shared the belief that the new technology could be improved to the point where microwave ovens would be able to do everything that conventional ovens could, but faster and with lower energy consumption. But even with the introduction and subsequent improvement of 'browning' and other advanced features, microwaved meats still tasted like they had been boiled, and homemade breads looked like they had been run through a dishwasher. And given those unappetizing outcomes, many consumers all but gave up on microwave ovens for roasting and baking and began using them for a variety of special purposes, such as thawing frozen foods, reheating leftovers, and heating up frozen dinners – and, of course, making popcorn.

'A man seldom thinks with more earnestness of anything than he does of his dinner.'
– Dr Samuel Johnson (1709–1784), English author, critic and lexicographer

In consequence, as consumers gained a better understanding of the limits of the technology, *they* redefined the product concept. In their minds, the microwave oven had become a supplement to traditional kitchen ovens and ranges, not a replacement for them, and the desired product was smaller and simpler than the complex models being touted as the wave of the future. Yet the change was obscured for the US manufacturers by what they considered 'common sense': What American wouldn't want a microwave oven large enough to roast a turkey or a browning element for meats and breads?

When hot buttons shifts like these occur, companies that don't wish to change their product strategies have to accept smaller target markets. Amana acknowledged this trade-off when it explicitly chose to limit its market by refusing to make inexpensive appliances that might compromise its image as a high-end manufacturer. On the other hand, companies that are wrongly convinced that they have remained in sync with the evolving hot buttons of potential customers are likely to make disastrous investments based on overly optimistic forecasts. This was the self-made trap into which Litton apparently fell as it continued to place its bets and investments on big, complicated, do-everything cooking appliances.

What's especially striking about Litton's choices, though, is that they were made in an environment littered with obvious indicators about the shift in customer hot buttons. Here are a just a few examples of how the press tried to sound the alarm:

- In 1978, the same year Litton pronounced its aim to be being 'king of the hill' in microwave ovens, *Mart*, a trade publication, criticized the industry for its gamble on the replacement strategy. 'The fact is,' they wrote, 'that today's customers are buying top-end microwave models to supplement their basic cooking appliances – not to replace them.'

- In 1979, *The Wall Street Journal* chided manufacturers for trying 'to outglitter each other' with a variety of technological gimmicks. And, it warned, 'the gadgetry overwhelms some people,' including one man who commented, 'You have to be Thomas Edison to know how to use it.'

- In 1983, a similar theme was sounded by the industry publication *Merchandising Week*. Why, the editors asked, were manufacturers still organizing cooking schools on how to cook Thanksgiving dinner in a microwave oven? From their perspective, the automatic cooking codes and cooking sensors then being introduced were missing the market by a wide margin.

- As late as the end of 1986, *Consumer Reports* noted with dismay that the latest product introductions continued to reflect the 'manufacturers' persistent and possibly irrational desire to have the microwave oven replace the range.'

In the end, thinking about the microwave oven as a replacement rather than as an adjunct led to unattractive investments in costly, fancy features that customers didn't use, and therefore refused to pay for. It also helped to create the opportunity for Japanese and, later, Korean manufacturers to offer the smaller, simpler, cheaper machines that customers sought.

Markets mutate;
no advance notice provided

Markets mutate. They shift, combine, divide, combust spontaneously, and sometimes go supernova, leaving black holes in corporate coffers. Driving such diverse changes are alterations in the customers' hot buttons: which customers want what, how much they want it, and why. But when customers alter their hot buttons, they vote at the cash register rather than make formal announcements. And when vendors don't detect these changing *who*s, *what*s, *how-much*s and *why*s, as happened in the microwave oven industry, they can find themselves encumbered by outdated or just flat-out incorrect beliefs about the products they sell and the markets in which they participate.

This problem is compounded when the buyers and sellers come from different cultures or different countries. That was the experience of US investment firms that exported syndicated real estate deals to the Japanese market during the hot 1980s – and found little demand because the Japanese concept of real estate at the time was owning a *particular* piece of property, not sharing in the proceeds of a *portfolio* of properties. Nike had a similar experience when it tried to export its in-your-face, antiestablishment message outside of North America in the late 1990s. Aside from the irony of a $9 billion company playing the role of *enfant terrible*, the message was seen as more 'ugly American' than cutting edge hipster.

Or consider the agony that Mercedes Benz experienced when it set about to regain the US luxury car market in the 1990s. The market intelligence was clear: prospective buyers in the US wanted cup holders in their cars. Not only would meeting this desire require a costly dashboard redesign, the whole notion of drinking coffee (or any other beverage) in a car was repugnant to the German engineers. What kind of people would use their automobiles as roving lounges? Evidently, people who could – and would – buy Mercedes Benz cars. As company insiders tell the story, ultimately the designers held their noses and made the change – and the new cup holders became one of the many reasons that American luxury car buyers returned to Mercedes.

But even when the cultural issues are minor, understanding the basic *why*s of customer behavior can elude companies that are otherwise superbly positioned to capitalize on shifting customer desires. For example:

- How could Digital Equipment Company have missed the emerging market for personal computers? Apple created a mass of customers eager for their own computing power; Ken Olsen, CEO of Digital, declared the PC to be a fad. The company later entered the market, but only after a variety of competitors had established commanding positions.

- How could Nestlé (Nescafé), General Foods (Maxwell House), and Procter & Gamble (Folger's) have missed the emerging market for gourmet coffees? Starbucks and a gaggle of other smaller entrepreneurs shined the spotlight on customers thirsty for a better cup of joe. Nonetheless, Nestlé, GF, and P&G, perhaps hesitant to move to the higher-cost Arabica beans that give gourmet coffees their flavor and kick, allowed the upstarts to create and then hold onto the fast-growing premium segment of the market.

• How could Heinz, Del Monte, and Hunt's have missed the emerging market for tomato-based salsas? The Hispanic population in the US was growing as was Gringo interest in Mex-Tex cooking. Notwithstanding the trends, the obvious players hung back and let lesser known upstarts storm – and capture – the grocery shelves.

As you review these situations, note that none of them required leaps of faith or extraordinary vision to imagine the market that didn't exist at the time. Nor did they require the kind of quantum leap in company strategy that was involved in the shift from vacuum tubes to transistors in electronic devices. Quite the contrary; each represented expansion into territories that were clearly visible and closely related to current operations of the market leaders. Yet in each case, as customer needs and wants began to shift, the only advantage held by the upstarts was that they saw the shifts – or helped to create the shifts – before the dominant players woke up to the opportunities at hand.

Of course, it's easy to use 20/20 hindsight to point out how companies have bungled golden opportunities; every company makes poor judgment calls at one time or another. But since all strategies are based on some implicit understanding of the 'right' product, such misreads of customer hot buttons can lead to elaborate plans based on weak foundations, just as Litton demonstrated in the microwave oven market. Or, going back to Boyd's OODA Loop, all other things being equal, if your observations are wrong, everything you do based on these observations is doomed.

Part two
A fistful of *why*s:
some 'why experiments'

One way to reduce the incidence and magnitude of incorrect observations is to ask 'why' customers do what they do, so you can get a clearer understanding of what the customer hot buttons are or could be. I call these the 'why experiments.' There are many ways to structure such investigations; four that I like in particular include thought experiments, live experiments, can-opener experiments, and trade-off experiments. All of them can be important, because 'why' gives predictive power: the more you know *why* customers do what they do, the more accurately you can predict *what* they will do given various circumstances. Or as a portfolio manager who consistently beats the market once told me, 'I look for anomalies, and try to figure out why they occurred. And once I know that, I know where I'm going to place my bets.'

'They who dream by day are cognizant of many things which escape those who only dream by night.'
– Edgar Allan Poe (1809–1849), American poet, critic and fiction writer

1. The thought experiments:
a penny for your musings

At a dinner party, someone once asked Andre Heiniger, then managing director of the Rolex watch company, 'How's the watch industry?' Heiniger's huffy response? 'Rolex is not in the watch business. We are in the luxury business.'

I've always thought that this was a great example of someone who knows what his product is. But it's interesting to think how the people at Rolex might have come to this understanding. Not so long ago, a Rolex watch represented the ultimate in timekeeping technology, from its self-winding mechanism (a revolutionary feature at a time when watches required daily manual winding) to its performance under water. One of the clearest memories of a friend of mine, who was a child in London during World War II and is now a proud Rolex wearer, is of Royal Air Force flyers, scooped out of the English Channel after having bailed out of their damaged aircraft, their Rolex watches intact and still ticking.

After the war came inexpensive watches from companies like Timex which flooded the market but couldn't touch a Rolex in accuracy. Several decades later came the quartz revolution, and with it, precision time pieces, great prices, and no-hassle maintenance. To get to Heiniger's product concept for Rolex watches, someone must have asked 'why': why do Rolex watches continue to sell when its accuracy comes close to (but neither equals nor exceeds) that of quartz timepieces which sell for a small fraction of the price – for which maintenance is both far less expensive and far less cumbersome?

'Why', in fact, is one of the most powerful questions a marketer or strategist can pose, because it paves the way for anticipating future changes in customer behavior. Why is it that we think we have the ultimate product, and yet customers are still flocking to our competitors? What if it isn't just our marketing campaign, but something intrinsic to our product that our customers don't like? Or: why is it that this little product we have, the one that we pay virtually no attention to, continues to grow despite our neglect? What is the market telling us about the benefits our product provides versus those provided by the alternatives?

Or: why are customers doing things that don't fit our expectations? Think about women's dress shoes. Starting in the mid 1970s, when women were beginning to enter business and the professions in significant numbers, an explosion of books and articles describing how women should dress for their new careers hit the shelves in American bookstores. And, accordingly, more and more women did 'dress for success,' traipsing up and down streets across the US in their expensive silks and pearls – and ratty sneakers. In retrospect, the market question is obvious: Why would women who obviously took great pride in their appearance allow their self-image to stop at their ankles? Well, let's make some wild hypotheses. Older cities such as Boston have lots of cobblestone sidewalks, which do a great job of scuffing the heels of dress pumps. Rain and snow are also murder on leather shoes. Perhaps women carried their dress shoes to protect them from such extra wear and tear.

'The trick is to balance on the balls of your feet. It also helps to be in a situation where you don't have to walk.' – former fashion model, on wearing high-heeled dress pumps

And here's an even wilder idea, based on years of personal experience: traditional high heels hurt – especially when used for exotic purposes such as walking more than a block or standing for more than ten minutes. (If you don't believe me, take note of how often women slip their feet partially out of their shoes when seated in a restaurant, or at a conference table, or behind a desk.)

In 1987, one US company took aim at the sartorial curiosity. That was when US Shoe launched the Easy Spirit Dress Shoe line, with the tag line of 'looks like a pump, feels like a sneaker' – and television ads featuring women clad in scanty shorts, tee shirts, and Easy Spirit high heels ... playing an aggressive game of basketball. It was an ad that miffed some professional women, though not me as I was instantly convinced that if the models could play basketball in those heels without killing each other – or the producer of the spot – the shoes were worth trying. A number of other women reached the same conclusion, including one who confided to *The Wall Street Journal*: 'For the first time, I can walk ten blocks to a business lunch without freaking out.'

Shortly after the Easy Spirit launch, I found myself seated at a dinner next to the Executive Vice President for marketing for one of the world's major athletic shoe companies. We began to chat, and I asked him what he thought of the Easy Spirit product concept. Stupid idea, he told me, it will never work. Women like me would never buy them, he said – the need was illusory. And that ad! Sophisticated business women would surely be offended by the image of buffed and polished models playing B-Ball in high heels. Too bad. Easy Spirit experienced a 200 percent growth rate for the two years after its introduction, fueled in tiny part by the pair I was wearing at that dinner (and promptly showed to my dinner companion, thereby clearly convincing him of my preeminent status among the fashion-impaired).

The Easy Spirit march into the market for comfortable dress shoes for women didn't go as far as I had hoped, perhaps because its corporate parent, US Shoe, ran into troubles, limiting potential reinvestment in the business for a time. In addition, to my eye at least, the product line never went much beyond dowdy. As a result, though Easy Spirit pioneered the path, much of the potential market for really comfortable, really pretty dress shoes for women (and for men, I reckon – if you change the second descriptor from 'pretty' to 'handsome') remained open, creating an opportunity my dinner companion could have exploited on behalf of his company, had he been looking.

Thought experiments like these cost nothing – except the discomfort of thinking outside the normal business boundaries. But they can unlock new and better ways of understanding what a product is – either for the current vendors, or for new competitors eager to snag a portion of the market that present participants cannot, or will not, see.

2. The live experiments:
just do it

In the thought experiments, you ask why, and then develop or revise a product and launch it in the market. The live experiments require you to do just the opposite; launch first, question second.

For example, a common Japanese method of market research is to launch vast numbers of products and then cull the winners – often introducing products first at home and taking the survivors abroad. This in fact appears to be the approach taken by the Japanese manufacturers during the microwave oven wars – but not by Litton, which was certain that its familiarity with the home market formed an unbeatable advantage. Or as the company's vice president of marketing declared in 1982, 'Domestic firms can do a superior job in marketing and understanding the consumer, so [we] are not under any handicap.'

That may have been the prevailing belief at Litton, but it certainly seems that revising strategy based on sales numbers provided the non-US competitors with key information that the Americans missed. So even though the Japanese manufacturers may not have done much in the way of formal market research, the monthly figures coming back from the States told them what they needed to know: US customers wanted smaller and simpler machines and therefore these were the models that received subsequent investment and attention from the Japanese producers. Meanwhile, as Japanese market share began to grow, Litton delayed changing course, either because it misunderstood which products were fueling its competitors' success, or because it neglected to ask why the success was occurring at all. In the fight for share in the microwave oven market, ongoing live experimentation by market outsiders ultimately overwhelmed the local advantage of the home team.

Microsoft also uses live experiments to test and improve certain products. Former Microsoft insider Julie Bick says that when the company launched the first version of its networking product, Windows for Workgroups, management knew the product would provide only, in Bick's words, 'some' of the solutions its prospective customers were seeking. 'Rather than waiting until all issues could be solved,' she explains, 'the product went to market, helping users with a subset of their problems and paving the way for feedback on what to solve next, and how to prioritize resources based on customer needs.' Customers captive to Microsoft will not be surprised by the disclosure – though they may feel their tempers rising just (or more than just) a bit. From the company's point of view, though, ongoing feedback from disgruntled users has been quite valuable and, in the case of Windows for Workgroups, went directly into the then-ongoing development for Windows 95.

Or, going back to Pepsi, John Sculley's home-use study of several decades ago became a live experiment, but only because Sculley was flexible enough to view it that way. But whether your industry involves microwaves or microcomputers, soft drinks or software, the underlying logic is the same: watch what customers actually do in a live situation, figure out what hot buttons are driving their behavior, and then adjust your strategy accordingly – one way to use the OODA Loop to create and modify a corporate strategy.

3. The can-opener experiments: just ask why

Sometimes a faster way to find out why prospective customers are doing what they are doing is simply to ask them. Which, of course, is what focus groups, among other market research techniques, are all about. The problem, though, is how you ask. Too often, standard questions evoke rote answers, obscuring the data you really need to uncover the true real hot buttons.

'I base my fashion sense on what doesn't itch.'
– Gilda Radner, American Comedian

Let's go back to women's shoes. I'm fairly certain that if you assembled a focus group of working women and asked the participants what they want in dress shoes, you'd likely hear about styling, durability and color. Now, imagine what would happen if you asked the participants to imagine that their feet could talk and having their feet respond to the question. Then I'd bet that you'd be greeted by something on the order of 'Get me out of these torture chambers!', and that you would then hear more about pain and contortions than about lines and elegance.

Or consider the company that developed a better bug spray. The effectiveness of the spray came from the delayed-action properties of the product: because the compound was lethal but didn't kill the bugs on contact, its effect multiplied as each contaminated bug greeted, and thereby infected, its friends and relatives. Despite its greater effectiveness, the product didn't sell as well as expected. Why? One reason was that if the customers didn't actually see the bugs die, they weren't sure that the product really worked. Psychological research at a second bug-killer company provides another possible reason: Customers saw the bugs as their enemy and wanted to see them die. No dead bugs, no repeat sale.

In fact, terrible pun aside, I have found that asking customers what 'bugs' them can be one of the most effective ways to elicit the customer information you need to make reality-based market decisions. That was the experience of GTE some years ago when the company decided to supplement its rigorous periodic customer-satisfaction testing with less structured focus groups. The regular testing consistently showed that GTE's telephone customers were highly satisfied with the appearance of the company's employees and with the range of services available. But in the focus groups, the customers revealed that their primary concerns were maintenance hours, reliability in transmission quality, and speed in emergency situations – categories not included in the customer satisfaction instruments.

The difference between structured questions like 'Are you satisfied with the range of services we offer?' and unstructured ones like 'What bugs you about this kind of product?' can be the difference between marginally useful data and data that can change a market – if you choose to pay attention. Then, once you loosen the question enough to be able to allow customers to tell you in their own way why they do what they do and how they feel about it, the logical next steps quickly come clear.

Remember the swimsuit research done in 1987 by SWIM – the Swimsuit Manufacturers' Association, mentioned in Chapter 1? It seems to me that the 'so-what' should have been immediately evident: help women look better in swimsuits (or at least, feel like they look better), and they'll buy more swimsuits. But in fact it took almost a decade until the manufacturers got the idea and finally began to offer suits cut less high on the hip, sized by bra size rather than by dress size, and made with fabrics that can conceal, pull in, and push up. Models in the *Sports Illustrated* annual swimsuit issue may not need these enhancements, but let's face it: supermodel Tyra Banks would look great in a modified potato sack; what about the average woman who is at least four inches shorter than Banks – and forty pounds heavier?

4. The trade-off experiments: cole slaw ... or fries?

Let's say you and a friend are planning your annual monthly dinner get-together. This time you're meeting in a city where you both have meetings, but where you are both first-time visitors. Your friend has researched the restaurant scene, and has picked out four restaurants he sees as the leading candidates for the meal. Being a little compulsive, he has sent you a letter with four cards, each in a different color, and each with a description of one of the restaurants. In his letter, he has asked you to rank the four cards, with #1 being the one you like the most, and #4 being the one you like the least. He has told you that he will call the restaurants for reservations in the order you indicate, trying #2 only if #1 is booked, and so on. All the restaurants offer the same general style of cuisine, and the prices are about the same at all four.

These are the four cards he has sent you. The stars, where given, are on a five point scale, and came from a local newspaper's restaurant reviews.

Yellow:
pretty good food (***)
good ambiance (*****)
no music
great desserts (****)

Red:
fantastic food (*****)
really crummy ambiance (*)
recorded classical music
okay desserts (***)

Green:
good food (****)
terrific ambiance (*****)
recorded classical music
terrible desserts (*)

Purple:
mediocre food (**)
okay ambiance (***)
live pop music
fantastic desserts (*****)

If you oblige your friend in his compulsiveness, you will make his task of restaurant selection easier. You might also give him insights that he could use if you meet for dinner in yet another city, simply because the order in which you ranked the cards provides a window onto your decision weights about restaurants. The cards would have been useful in showing your hot buttons – the variables to which you give disproportionate weight.

Now think about trying to provide a good deal to a group of people, each of whom may have their own hot buttons. What do you do? This is where conjoint or trade-off research can be useful as a way to take this murky situation and cause clear patterns to emerge. It works by having respondents rank a group of products, usually in order of likelihood of purchase. Each of these products is composed of a set of attributes and each attribute is varied in a systematic way, just as the four cards in the restaurant example were, though in a real conjoint test, the respondents are presented with more choices, typically either on cards or via a computer. The choices made by all the respondents become the input to a multiple regression calculation, the results of which (essentially the coefficients of the regression equation) provide a high level of detail on the decision weights customers apply to the attributes included in the test.

This level of detail isn't required in all situations, or even most. But it is invaluable when making product design and delivery decisions that will be difficult to reverse, or where time lost to make product fixes will be time used to the advantage of a competitor. If you were designing microwave ovens in the 1970s, for example, what was the importance of 'easy to use' versus inclusion of a browning element that would make the product (somewhat) more suitable for baking bread or broiling meats? (Notice, however, that a conjoint study that asked customers to make trade-offs only amongst a variety of high-tech options would be a classic example of GIGO research: garbage in, garbage out.) Or, if you are planning to cut costs tomorrow, would your customers prefer the continued operation of your central technical service staff but a reduced delivery schedule, or the other way around? For questions like these, in which guessing wrong could be an expensive proposition, it's particularly important to make sure that your company's design trade-offs are a good fit with the customer's purchase trade-offs. Otherwise, you may find that you have designed yourself into a market decline.

'Love never dies of starvation, but often of indigestion.'
– Ninon de Lenclos (1620–1705), French woman of society

In all cases, though, the critical task is to find a way to test whether the way you see your product matches what the market really wants. The fact that you believe that of course your product passes the hot buttons test is only normal; your competitors likely feel exactly the same way about their products. But as we all know, customers seem to throw the occasional spanner in the works – without either notice or explanation. So your love of your product notwithstanding, it's your choice: either test how well what you provide really matches what the customer wants – or let your competitors do it for you.

• • •

When Amsterdam's Schiphol executive Aad Kieboom got the chance to give a quote to *The Wall Street Journal*, this is what he said:

It improves aim. If a man sees a fly, he aims at it.

Kieboom was describing Schiphol's habit of etching the outline of a fly in every urinal in the airport. The result is men's rooms across the airport that are cleaner than their counterparts in other airports around the world. Kieboom and his Dutch colleagues say that, in their tests, adding flies to the urinals reduced 'spillage' by 80 percent. (This also helps to answer a universal question among women about why men, who can aim a basketball, satellite or laser with uncanny accuracy, cannot do the same with a commode.)

Do the flies make a difference that can be measured on the bottom line. I think the answer is 'yes.' Clean bathrooms are one of the thousands of details that makes Schiphol a model airport. And it was everything from clean bathrooms to effective gate logistics that, in 1997, led to a subsidiary of Dutch state-owned NV Luchthaven Schiphol being awarded a 30-year contract … to run the Arrivals Building of New York's John F. Kennedy Airport.

Regardless of the target, good aim is essential. And as Colonel Boyd pointed out, good aim starts with the ability to observe what is, rather than what is assumed to be.

Sin #3

Play to Win

*Business is in part a game ... a chess game.
I like playing chess.
I'm bad at it, but I like playing basketball.
Bill has other things he enjoys.
Business, we're actually pretty good at.*

– Steve Ballmer,
Executive Vice President, Microsoft.
Steve's score in 1997,
as measured by his equity in the company:
about $7,000,000,000.
Bill's: about $35,000,000,000.
(that's nine zeros, as in billions)

Signs when the company credo is to play to win ...
... but is aimed at the wrong game
with the wrong rules

- The company mascot should be 'the moving hockey stick' because improvement in performance for the products or services in question is always 'just around the corner.'

- A key product is losing share – relative to either industry sales or industry profits – and:

    - the loss is ignored since total sales are growing (though not as fast as industry sales);

    - the loss is attributed to the 'inevitable' result of new competition, and is then seen as acceptable and therefore as not really a problem after all;

    - no one inside the company can really explain why the loss has occurred, other than to blame it on 'exogenous factors' (read: 'conditions beyond our control' ... and 'therefore not our fault');

    - the market is redefined so the loss is no longer apparent – providing immediate relief to all (and improved air cover for the competition).

- Time-honored rules of thumb about how to attract and retain customers keep being applied, even though feedback from the market suggests that the wrong thumbs are being used.

- Management, certain that the pricing strategies of key competitors are 'irrational' and that these companies must be losing money, decides to:

  ○ wait until the opponents regain their senses and raise their prices (... but they don't);

  ○ cut prices drastically to stem share losses or to 'discipline' industry renegades (... but the company can't make money at the new prices, and the renegades don't seem to learn their lesson); or

  ○ both, sequentially.

- Cost cutting is ordered to fix the problem, and yet, somehow, the new cost structure and associated lower prices don't bring customers back to the product or service.

- The most significant term in the company's economic model, buried somewhere deep within the plans, is the one that states: 'suddenly, a miracle occurs.'

- The more you think about it, the more you conclude that Boyd's OODA Loop has been transformed into the company's DOOM Loop; every action either seems to have no beneficial effect or seems to worsen the situation.

'We don't have a plan. We make strategy through conversation.' That's what a senior executive of a major European company told me, as his colleagues nodded in agreement. At first I was startled. Then I realized that he was exactly right: almost all companies make their largest strategic decisions 'through conversation'; that is, through discussion. The exceptions are those organizations in which top managers have effectively abdicated the strategy-setting decisions to outsiders or, at the other extreme, those in which the CEOs, often entrepreneur-founders, confer with no one but themselves. At most, though, and regardless of how the process is described officially, shifts in a company's real strategy emerges through ongoing conversation. That's how the people with the authority to take big decisions come to working conclusions about whether and how to make major changes in the company's game plan, the rules by which to play – or even in the choice of game itself.

'Strategy is not the consequence of planning but rather the opposite: its starting point.' – Henry Mintzberg (b. 1939), McGill University

Some of these conversations take place in formal, scheduled meetings: departmental or team working sessions; presentations by taskforces or consultants; strategy reviews with senior management. Others are somewhat formal but more fragmented in time: requests for information and deliveries of information that go down, up, and through the organization. And by far the most common kinds of conversations are the informal, often serendipitous or accidental ones that can take place anywhere, anytime: at tradeshows or in elevators; over dinners or in taxi cabs; at the end of some other meeting or over the course of a long plane ride.

But no matter how and where these conversations are conducted, it's the substance that matters. That's why, as explored in this chapter, it's critical to structure these conversations around fundamental questions: what game you think you're playing, by what rules, and why you think you'll achieve your goals if you continue with the current playbook. These kinds of questions often require more detailed analysis than indicated in the previous two chapters, which means you may have to get your hands dirtier in the data than you're used to, especially if you sit high up in your company's power structure. But they're also the kinds of questions that can help you see when you're about to hurtle headlong into a competitive dog-fight – as well as when you have the chance to create new game spaces that others don't yet see.

Part one
Strategy as prediction ...
... based on a set of beliefs

Strategy is prediction, based on a set of beliefs and leading to action. Your budgets and pro formas show the predictions you've made. Your actions show the beliefs you hold – about the competitive game you are or will be playing and the associated rules and conditions of that game. Beliefs about the current game drive day-to-day operating decisions regarding what benefits to give customers, at what price, and with what internal cost structure. In the same way, beliefs about tomorrow's game drive investment decisions aimed at changing the company's future position on any or all of these three dimensions of benefits, price, and costs.

Take a look at your own budgets and investment plans; what do they indicate about the game you think your company needs to play to achieve its goals? If you do a little digging, you may find some surprising answers about what you keep telling yourself is important (for example, innovation and new product development) and what your *real* strategy is (for example, further cost-cutting and endless modification of an old product line). You may also find that you then have a more difficult time figuring out *why* your decisions are falling into this pattern.

One reason for the gap is that while most companies spend enormous time putting together their numbers and arguing about pricing strategies and cost structures, many never really examine the basic beliefs on which these operating and investment decisions are predicated. Then, when performance is better than they had ever dared hoped, they may not be aware enough of what they did right to replicate and adjust it in the future. Conversely, when what was promised exceeds what was delivered, there may be so little understanding of what caused the failure that the company either continues to repeat the same mistakes with small variations or moves directly into full-fledged panic mode as it seeks some 'silver bullet' to achieve the performance it projected. Consider the following two product launches, separated by about 40 years, which illustrate the predicament.

A tale of two launches:
The Model 95 versus the Spectra

On November 27, 1948, two employees of a struggling start-up prepared to execute the entire launch strategy for their company's new product. The venue for the event: a small alcove in Boston's Jordan Marsh department store. Back at what passed for corporate headquarters – which in fact was a grungy warehouse across the river in East Cambridge, Massachusetts – everyone wondered whether there would be any takers for the product, a new camera for general consumer use. A key concern was the camera's selling price which, at $95.00, seemed preposterous when compared to the $2.75 price tag on Kodak's Baby Brownie, then the category leader. Though at the last minute company executives lowered the new camera's price to $89.75, they remained nervous that the price was still way too high to attract enough customers to make the venture viable.

They needn't have worried. Within minutes of the first demonstration of the 'Polaroid Land Camera Model 95,' a crowd formed in the store's cramped camera department, with people pushing and shoving to get a look at the world's first instant camera – and to purchase one on the spot. Asked by the store's assistant manager to return the next morning, the two Polaroid reps explained that they could arrive no earlier than 2 p.m. – the 56 cameras that the Jordan Marsh customers had just purchased represented the company's entire inventory. Prior to that morning, Polaroid had hoped that, with luck, all 56 could be sold by Christmas; now, after frantic calls back to East Cambridge, camera production had been kicked into overdrive, with more cameras to be ready the next afternoon. And so began Polaroid's phenomenal entry into the photography market.

Nearly 40 years later, in 1986, Polaroid staged another memorable product launch, this time for Spectra, its newest instant camera and film system. The event was held at the Century Plaza Hotel in Los Angeles with all the fanfare of a major movie opening – blaring music, twirling dancers, and a two-story replica of the new camera. Polaroid management predicted that Spectra would, in the words of company chairman William J. McCune, 'make a major restatement of instant photography and reposition instant photography in the eyes of the consumer.' Accordingly, upwards of $40 million was earmarked for the first year's advertising budget. But despite strong managerial commitment and major marketing bucks, Spectra sputtered; according to *Business Week*, first-year sales hit only two-thirds to three-quarters of management's projections (500,000–600,000 versus 800,000), with second-year sales declining 50 percent from there.

> 'I believe quite simply that the small company of the future will be as much a research organization as it is a manufacturing company, and that this new kind of company is the frontier for the next generation.'
> – Edwin Land, founder of Polaroid, in a paper written in 1944

The key numbers serve as an interesting comparison. The Model 95 carried a price tag that was thirty-three times that of the most popular amateur camera then on the market, was launched on a shoestring, and created a sensation. The highly advanced Spectra was priced at parity with inexpensive 35-millimeter cameras, was launched on a mega-budget – and yet, according to most analysts, was a flop. Why?

Of strategists and astrologers ...
... and the business of predicting – and creating – the future

One way to answer this question is to go back to the beliefs on which the two launches were based. For many people, though, identifying such core beliefs is a difficult process: actions and projections are what managers talk about; beliefs and predictions are topics for fortune tellers and astrologers. But if I'm correct that strategy is prediction based on a set of beliefs, then identifying underlying beliefs is essential to making good strategy. Which brings us back to the acid tests introduced in Chapter 1 – hot buttons, good deal, profit engine, and morphing chessboard – and the questions posed in Chapter 2 about what your products provide versus what your target customers want. In combination, these queries can help force out the covert certainties that are driving your organization's real strategy. Specifically, they require you to be explicit about what you believe to be:

- the size and trajectory of the potential market you are trying to reach, and why;

- the benefits, prices, and costs of your products versus those of your competitors and other alternatives available to your target customers;

- how these benefits, prices, costs might shift over time, and who might cause these shifts;

- other shifts that might take place that could affect the market (for example: changes in regulation, new findings from the scientific community, or shifts in supply); and

- the kinds of impacts these dynamics could have on your revenues and profits.

In most cases, I find that the fastest and most effective way to start is to take a quick pass the acid tests, using your working assumptions, best guesses, and easily accessible data in the areas just listed as the initial inputs. But if you do so, be aware that you may see some significant deviations from what you expected. It's one thing to assume, in the abstract, that your product provides 'the best deal' for your target customers. It's quite another to have to explain why you hold this belief if, for example, your own data indicate that your product offers only a slight edge over a competitor's but at a huge price premium, or if your product is losing share while an 'inferior' product from a competitor continues to break sales records.

A word of warning is therefore in order: pursuing the acid tests, even using your own assumptions about benefits, price and costs as part of the initial input, can lead to unsettling insights. This is especially true if you're already 'sure' that you have a good product, at a fair price, with an appropriate cost structure. But these are also the insights that can be vital to your success, by helping you to anticipate likely customer or competitor reaction more accurately. And, at the least, such insights can also help explain why past predictions failed, so you can increase the odds that you don't fall into the same trap again. Which returns us to the fabulous world of fun photography.

'If a man can write a better book, preach a better sermon, or make a better mousetrap than his neighbor, though he build his house in the woods, the world will make a beaten path to his door.'
– Ralph Waldo Emerson (1803–1882), American author and philosopher

Mousetrap economics: A second look at the Model 95 of 1948 versus the Spectra of 1986

Ralph Waldo Emerson was right: Build a better mousetrap and the world will beat a path to your door. But what Emerson didn't say is that this clearly wonderful outcome depends on the price you charge for your mousetrap relative to all the other alternatives available to your customers. This may all seem perfectly obvious, except that in a significant number of cases, even when the company correctly understands that its new contraption or service is superior to the other alternatives, it still can't price the offering high enough to cover total costs yet low enough to attract buyers. As inventors, investors, and assorted others have learned to their sorrow, a better mousetrap doesn't necessarily lead to a profitable business proposition.

And that's precisely the point illustrated by the two Polaroid launches. In 1948, when Polaroid introduced the Model 95, customers saw a good deal – even a great deal – despite the huge price tag. The reason was simple. In comparison to the other amateur cameras then available, the Model 95 provided the best combination of image quality and ease of use, in part due to the camera's significant simplification of the photographic tasks of selecting apertures and shutter speeds. It also provided a previously inconceivable benefit that became an instant hit: instant photographs. Imagine being able to see any photo only minutes after it was shot – at a time when your next best alternative required finishing the entire roll of film, making a special trip to a post office or a photo-finisher, and then waiting for days until you could actually see the prints.

But the competitive landscape in which Polaroid launched Spectra was quite different, in two key respects. First was relative image quality. Polaroid executives told the press that Spectra could produce photographs 'comparable in quality to [those] taken with inexpensive 35-millimeter cameras.' Supporting this belief, they said, was five years of market research. Yet the press didn't buy it, and neither did consumers. *Business Week* stated flatly that 35 mm cameras produced 'higher quality prints' than Spectra. Stan Grossfield, *Boston Globe* photography editor, focused his concerns about relative image quality on the technical side, noting that 'Spectra is competing with many Japanese 35 mm cameras having a similar price tag yet superior optics… [and] lenses that are much faster.'

The second difference, the relative value of sixty-second photographs, was perhaps even more troublesome. In 1948, instant was magic. But in 1986, with the prevalence of one-hour processing, not to mention the emergence of camcorders, traditional photography had become 'almost instant.' And though Spectra was priced at parity with its 35 mm competitors, the film was not. As *Business Week* did the math, customers could not only get 'higher quality prints' from their 35 mm cameras, they could do so 'at about half the price' of a Polaroid photograph. Nonetheless, Polaroid's top managers must have believed that the instant benefit was extremely valuable; how else could they have thought that the Spectra camera-and-film system would meet their sales projections, given the 100 percent price premium they were charging on the photos themselves?

So it's true, Spectra was a wonderful camera, elegantly designed and a pleasure to use; relative to other instant cameras, nothing could compare to it. But other instant cameras weren't the competition; 35 mm cameras were, and, increasingly, camcorders too. And in 1986, unlike 1948, the best combination of image quality and ease of use in still photography had shifted decisively to 35 mm. Similarly, though the time from camera click to print for a 35 mm photo had been reduced from days to minutes, Polaroid's comparative price for its instant feature remained high. In consequence, with its benefits at its price, Spectra held poor odds for meeting McCune's goal of 'repositioning instant photography in the eyes of the consumer.' In a contest between management beliefs and market realities, the market always wins, no matter how strong the company credo of playing to win.

Part two
The role of doodles in strategy:
when a picture is worth a thousand words

One technique for identifying core beliefs, such as the ones that formed the foundation for the Spectra launch, and then for playing around with them a bit, are 'competitive-game maps.' These maps, which I described briefly in *Fad Surfing*, provide a visual way to present answers to the acid tests. To construct them, start with simple x-y graphs, using the x-axis to represent the benefits that customers seek, and the y-axis for both the price to customers and the costs to the company. The resulting maps are still just tools, of course, and not answers. Nonetheless, if you're willing to spend some time on them, they can be exceptionally helpful in forcing out assumptions, showing contradictions, highlighting threats, and identifying opportunities, even when done in very rough form, as the following example illustrates.

Autopsy in Marlboro country:
near death due to hypercompetition ...
... or unintentional suicide?

Figure 3.1 shows a highly simplified competitive-game map for Marlboro cigarettes in comparison to the generic, private label, and discount cigarette brands that were introduced into the US market in 1980. Typically on a competitive-game map, as on this one, you expect to see correspondingly higher product prices as you move from left to right on the x-axis. You also expect to see share gains for products sitting below the prevailing rough band of increasing prices for increasing benefit – or what we can call the 'good-deal band'; and conversely, share losses for those sitting above.

'I have every sympathy with the American who was so horrified by what he had read of the effects of smoking that he gave up reading.'
– Lord Conesford (1892–1974)

Now look at the map in Fig. 3.1. As you can see, over the period of 1980 to 1993, Marlboro's price increased by an average of 10 percent per year (as represented on the y-axis) while its benefit position remained approximately the same (as shown on the x-axis). Meanwhile, the low-end brands enjoyed less robust price increases at the same time that their position on the x-axis began to creep to the right, reflecting increased public confidence in the consistency and reliability of these market upstarts.

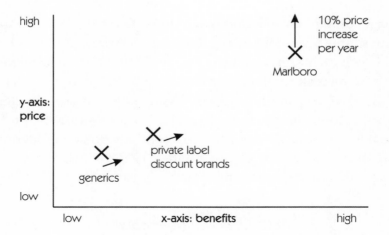

Fig. 3.1 Good-deal drift in the US cigarette market, 1980–1993.

Even a glance at the map shows the dilemma Marlboro was creating for itself: each year, smokers found that they had to pay more and more of a premium in price (the growing gap on the y-axis) to get less and less of a premium in benefits (the lessening gap on the x-axis). That meant it was highly likely, over time, that some customers were going to do the opposite of the old motto for Lucky Strikes cigarettes: they were going to switch, rather than fight – which they in fact did do in accelerating numbers. The result should not have come as a shock. By 1993, the off-price labels had taken almost 40 percent of the US market.

Nor was this story of increasing gaps in price for decreasing gaps in benefits unique to Marlboro. Adrian Slywotzky, author of *Value Migration*, points out that in the US market, the average price premium for branded products over their generic alternatives went from 20 to 30 percent in 1980, to about 100 percent in 1990. Not surprisingly, almost all of these brands eventually found themselves in the same situation as Marlboro did in 1993, with mounting share losses and the unhappy choice of either protecting margins or regaining share. You can blame this on 'exogenous forces' if you wish ('for some reason, consumers don't

care about brands any more'), but I say competitive-game maps
– even ones rendered as simply as the one in Fig. 3.1 –
expose the real story.

Competitive-game maps like this can help clarify key
market dynamics and therefore improve the conversations through which strategies are created. Used on an
after-the-fact basis, they can aid in discovering why shifts
in margin and share occurred, an important step in break-
ing the cycle of continuing mistakes based on management beliefs that either have become outmoded or never
fit the market very well in the first instance. Similarly,
used on a prospective basis, they can aid in anticipating
likely next moves and reactions by both customers and
competitors. But before they can be used, they have to
be constructed, which in turn requires a few words here.

*'Perception is
strong and sight
weak. In strategy
it is important to
see distant things
as if they were
close and to take
a distanced view
of close things.'*
– Miyamoto
Musashi (1584–
1645)

Roughly right versus precisely wrong: figuring out how to frame the maps

Competitive-game maps are one of those business tools that require patience. And a large waste-paper basket. That's because
getting both the y-axis (price) and the x-axis (benefits) 'roughly
right' is as much an art as a science, and usually involves substantial trial and error.

For the y-axis, the tough issues include identifying and dis-
playing prices according to the implicit metrics customers use,
as well as making reasonable rough estimates of competitors'
costs relative to the benefits these alternatives provide. These
are matters that typically require effort upfront to frame the
questions correctly (for example, how customers calculate price),
and then additional time collecting and crunching the numbers.

And sometimes a fair amount of creativity is required as well.
For newspapers, for example, the y-axis for prices to advertisers
is clearly denominated in units of currency. But advertisers only

place adverts in newspapers if the papers consistently attract enough of the right readers. So when advertisers consider potential venues for their ads, are they more interested in the price readers pay in coins or in minutes? If I were an advertiser, I'd be interested in reader eyeball time, because the more eyeball time, the better the odds that the right eyes would see my ads. And for that reason, if I were a newspaper publisher, I'd want one version of the y-axis for readers to be denominated in time rather than cash.

'Many useful things turn out to be incalculable. This escapes the attention of bad economists, and drives good economists crazy.'
– Howard H. Stevenson, Harvard Business School

For the x-axis, though, the problem is almost the reverse. Here calculating a numerically denominated axis can obscure the very realities you need to see. This is counterintuitive to many people who, when confronted by numerical values on a y-axis, seem to fall instantly under the sway of some instinctive pull to create a numerical x-axis as well. But even if you have excellent data from a conjoint study, most companies don't have *all* the numbers needed to make the x-axis fully numeric – unless they either leave out some variables (especially the intangibles), or make up the numbers they need to fill the gaps. (Please don't laugh; I've seen very smart and honest people do both.)

For this reason, I've learned that in most cases the best way to construct the x-axis (benefits) of a game-map is take a more conceptual approach, along the lines of the schematic shown in Fig. 3.2.

Though this is a simplified way of modelling benefits from the customer's point of view, it still requires hard thinking about the component elements – the TTPs (tickets to play) and the

Fig. 3.2 Schematic for the x-axis of competitive-game maps.

various kinds of differentiators – and about how to combine the TTPs and differentiators into an x-axis that helps you make sense of the market. A bit more on these components for the constructing the x-axis follows.

The TTPs (tickets to play)

In the schematic shown in Fig. 3.2, the TTPs are the 'tickets-to-play.' TTPs are the features that all customers expect in a given segment; they are the 'must-haves' of the product. Alternately, if customers discover post-purchase that one of the expected TTPs is missing, expect that they will broadcast the mishap to other potential customers (even if you never hear about the complaint directly) and, if the problem persists, that they will defect to some other alternative. In addition, if you introduce a product to the market with many wonderful features but lacking the TTPs, you can bet that the product will fail; that's the territory indicated as '<TTP' on the far left of the schematic. In other words, no TTPs, no viable economic model.

In the hotel business, for example, pillows for each bed are an obvious TTP – which is probably why a travel writer for the *Boston Herald* was still complaining in print years after the fact about the resort hotel that refused him a pillow for the second bed in the room with the explanation, 'We're all out; everyone wanted one tonight.' Less obvious, perhaps, are the hair dryers in the bathroom and the complementary shampoos that have also become TTPs for mid-scale and up-scale hotels that cater to the business traveler. (You can check this for yourself; do you keep shampoo in your travel kit? If you do, is it because you prefer a certain brand, or because you assume that no shampoo will be provided by your hotel?) One important lesson about TTPs; like markets, they shift. What's a TTP today may have been a differentiator in the past (frequent flier programs for airlines), and vice versa (just about everything

'There is not much to say about most airplane journeys. Anything remarkable must be disastrous, so you define a good flight by the negatives ... you didn't crash, you didn't throw up, you weren't late, you weren't nauseated by the food.'
– Paul Theroux (b. 1941), American writer

else in air travel, including politeness, honesty about delays, modest leg room, or in-flight meal service that coincides with the times most folks have breakfast, lunch, and dinner).

The differentiators

On the right-hand side of Fig. 3.2, the 'diffs' are the 'differentiators.' These are the product attributes that distinguish one offering from another in a category, given that all the products provide the TTPs. As shown in Fig. 3.2, the differentiators can be loosely organized into groups. The first-level differentiators are the distinguishing features that many vendors offer, the second-level differentiators are those that only some vendors offer, and so on. Differentiators can be tangible or intangible. For US hotel chains competing for the business traveler, for example, a first-level differentiator may be a fitness center on premises, a second-level differentiator may be 24-hour room service or an in-room fax machine, while a third-level one may be the absolute consistency of the hotel chain's operations in making your stay as easy and hassle-free as possible, no matter what city or country you find yourself in.

In general, if all potential customers like all the differentiators, but not all of them can afford to purchase products with the full range of benefits, customers' selections of products will move both right and left on the x-axis – to the right, when they're willing to spend more to get more; to the left, when they can or must do with less. But not all customers like all differentiators. For this reason, I find it useful to think about differentiators as falling into three further categories: '+/+s', '+/=s', and '+/-s'.

- 'Plus/pluses' ('+/+s') are features that almost everyone tends to like, such as bathrobes in the rooms for hotels.

- 'Plus/equals' ('+/=s') are features that some customers value and will either pay extra for or shift their purchase in order to get, but that have little or no appeal to others and are therefore excluded from the good-deal calculations of this latter group. A fitness center in a hotel is a good example of a '+/=' in the lodgings business.

- 'Plus/minuses' ('+/-s') are those product elements that some people love – and other people hate; a loud and active bar/dance scene might appeal strongly to some travelers and be the last thing others want (especially if rooms near the bar aren't adequately soundproofed). The more '+/-s' a product has, the more likely it is that this product is part of a distinct segment that needs to be shown on a separate map.

If you categorize the TTPs and differentiators incorrectly, expect to see a market that behaves differently than you predicted, just as happened with Polaroid in a positive direction in the 1940s, and in a negative one the 1980s. Then you can decide either to try understand why – and possibly sacrifice cherished beliefs in the process – or, especially in those cases when the news is bad, to close your eyes while redoubling your efforts.

The Father Christmas approach to constructing the x-axis: make a list and check it twice

If you're willing to get your hands dirty in the data, the first step I recommend for creating the x-axis of a competitive-game map is to generate a list of the product elements for the product and the competing alternatives. At this stage, there's no need to be discriminating about the type of element or the order in which they are listed – tangible versus intangible, attribute versus benefit, basic versus esoteric, in-use versus pre-use or post-use. Just get them all down on paper. This will save time in generating the lists and free you from endless debate on whether a product element such as 'clean bathroom' is an 'attribute' or a 'benefit' for a hotel chain.

If your company sells to other enterprises who then sell to the end users, first try to construct a rough map for your customer's customer, and after that, one for your direct customer. This will allow you to see the TTPs and differentiators for serving your customers more accurately – and, on occasion, to see them in a totally new way. For example, in the newspaper business, advertising revenues from supermarkets have been declining, based on the belief among supermarket executives that their customers shop primarily on price and therefore want 'everyday low pricing' rather than the 'high-low pricing'. But consider the findings of Stephen Hoch, a professor at the University of Chicago. His research shows that supermarkets using high-low pricing have slightly lower revenues than those following the everyday-low-pricing approach – and significantly higher profits. What if the explanatory variable is that the thrill of the chase – finding special bargains – provides psychic benefits to certain customers? Then there could be additional profits for the taking for all the parties in the system (including, in this case, newspapers if they can convince their advertisers about Professor Hoch's findings).

Once you have the list of benefits in hand – either for your customer or for your customer's customer – the next step is to categorize the items as either TTPs or differentiators. As you identify the TTPs, remember that tickets-to-play can vary by location for the same product (bedside alarm clocks are TTPs for any business hotel in the US but not in some European countries), and that even within a market TTPs can move to the right on the x-axis and become differentiators or slide to the left and become TTPs. Also remember the 'invisible' variables that are the TTPs in some categories: compatibility with dominant operating systems for software; distribution for many packaged goods. Then, for the differentiators, the task is to take a first cut at making rough categories by level (first-level differentiators, second-level differentiators, and so on) and also by type (+/+, +/=, or +/-). I recommend saving these initial worksheets because, as explained later in this chapter, when the maps tell stories that don't match the facts about shifts in share of industry sales or profits, the problem often resides in a miscast x-axis.

What does all this look like in a real example? Let's go back to Marlboro. I see the TTP for cigarettes as 'a nicotine delivery system in smokable form.' I see the primary differentiators as related to the two functions that brands can fulfill: (1) making promises (in this case, to assure customers about the consistency and reliability of the product) and, (2) broadcasting information (in this case, to allow customers to transmit a desired image about themselves to themselves and to others by virtue of their use of the product). I therefore see the first-level differentiator for Marlboro as 'brand-as-promise,' where the promise is consistency of taste, packaging, and production standards; and the second-level differentiator as 'brand-as-image,' with the Marlboro cowboy in all his glory. Using this thinking as a basis for a simplified x-axis, and mapping only Marlboro and its low-end rivals, the revised competitive-game map in the cigarette market might look like the one shown in Fig. 3.3.

'I am irresistible, I say, as I put on my designer fragrance. I am a merchant banker, I say, as I climb out of my BMW. I am a juvenile lout, I say, as I down a glass of extra strong lager. I am handsome, I say, as I don my Levi's jeans.'
– John Kay, Oxford University

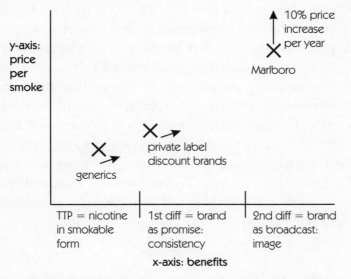

Fig. 3.3 Competitive-game map for Marlboro cigarettes, US market, 1980–1993.

You might see the x-axis for cigarettes somewhat differently. However you see it, though, the key is to use a schematic that shows your assumptions clearly. In this case, as in many in business analysis, roughly right in words is more useful than falsely precise in figures.

Market distortions:
too narrow versus too broad

Price/performance graphs, in which price (e.g. price of a microprocessor) is mapped against a uniform scale of performance (e.g. millions of instructions per second), have been around for a long time. But as the Marlboro example shows, competitive-game maps differ in several respects from the price-performance view of a market. One difference is that on the y-axis of a competitive-game map, price is given for the entire package and not just a single component (e.g. price of the fully loaded PC plus access to service, not just the processor). Another is that the x-axis of a competitive-game map is given in words rather than numbers, because it includes not only performance variables, which are easy to quantify, but also other tangible and intangible features that aren't easily converted to numbers but still have major influence on customers' purchase decisions. A third difference is that whereas price/performance graphs are by definition the same for everyone, in competitive-game maps both the y-axis and the x-axis can vary by groups of customers. For the x-axis, the issues can be particularly tricky. Here the key questions are whether the x-axis is drawn too narrowly, leaving out key competitors and therefore key threats, or alternately, too broadly, thereby overestimating the game space.

Too Narrow?

When companies define their markets too narrowly, the cause usually begins with defining the TTPs too narrowly in the first place, which in turn leads to ignoring a whole subset of important competitors. In the 1980s, for example, had you thought the TTP for cigarettes – and virtually all packaged grocery goods – was being a branded product (because that's what the TTP always had been), you would have excluded the generics as 'not part of our market.' In consequence, you wouldn't have been able to see the growing 'value gap' between the branded goods and their lower-brow brethren – and the resulting customer migration path.

Or consider what happened to the breakfast cereals producers in the United States during the mid-1990s. Benchmarking their rising retail prices only against each other, they saw their good-deal positions as stable. Customers begged to differ, however, and made their resentment clear by shifting some of their cereal purchases not only to the generics, but also to alternate fast breakfast foods – bagels, muffins, pop tarts and the like – that provided better combinations of benefits and price. When the cereal manufacturers woke up and rolled back their prices, their sales shot up. In this case, implicitly thinking about the breakfast TTP as something on the order of 'branded grain in the box,' rather than a broader category such as 'quick and easy,' obscured the real dynamics of the market.

Too Broad?

Conversely, when companies conceive of their potential markets as larger than they actually are, a common source of the misread is getting the TTPs right – and then overestimating the universality of appeal for their differentiators. If you think you have a set of differentiators that are '+/+s' – when your customers see them as '+/-s' – you will radically overestimate your market. That's what happened in the microwave oven industry, as well as in countless other electronic products that went to market with a panoply of advanced bells and whistles – whether the customer wanted them or not.

> 'I hate those heated toilet seats they have in Japan. The Japanese love them. But to me they feel like an army has been there just before me.'
> – European executive previously posted in Japan

Another, more dangerous, way to overestimate a market is to misunderstand the TTPs required, and therefore not realize that the product lacks some or all of the TTPs, or meets the TTPs for a smaller segment of the market than assumed in the pro formas, or can only offer the TTPs for the desired market at exorbitant costs (and therefore exorbitant price). These are surprisingly common problems in new enterprises, as well as for established companies introducing new products. For purposes of illustration, let's go back to Spectra and Fig. 3.4, which shows two possible ways of graphing Spectra's position at the time of its launch.

These two versions of the competitive-game map for Spectra have different definitions and scales for both the x-axis and y-axis. Taken individually, they also tell diametrically opposed stories. According to Version 1, Spectra has a shot at an attractive market: though customers might vary in how they calculate the

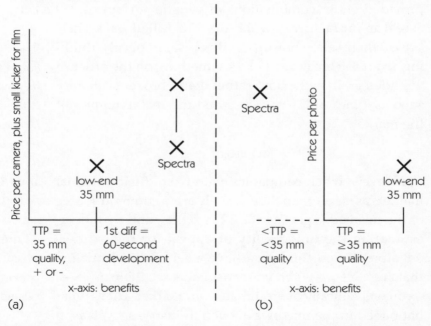

(a)   (b)

Fig. 3.4 (a) Version 1 of Spectra's position in the casual-use market at time of launch. (b) Version 2 of Spectra's position in the casual-use market at time of launch.

price of the system, the bottom line is that they will get more from the Spectra than from a low-end 35 mm device. Version 2, however, prophesizes a tale of woe: Spectra costs more but doesn't even deliver the TTPs – and therefore will have no market at all.

Now consider an alternate interpretation: the two charts need to be looked at together, because the actual market was characterized by two segments, one that looked something like Version 1 in Fig. 3.4, and the other something like Version 2. In this case, you can see that if you assumed the whole market looked like Version 1, you would have overestimated Spectra's potential, especially if the Version 2 segment was much larger than the one shown in Version 1. The divergence in these interpretations brings us back to a core use of competitive-game maps: the identification of the 'killer assumptions.' These are the assumptions that, if wrong, could land the company in a world of hurt – and that therefore, no matter how self-evident they seem to be, can benefit the most from tough challenge and hard testing.

Part three
The art of conversation:
using doodles to tell stories

One of the things that I like about competitive-game maps is that it's tough to construct them without making your assumptions explicit about benefits and price, as already discussed. But what I like even more are the tales these maps can tell. When compared to past performance, these stories can help you retest the analytic inputs used to construct the maps, examine prevailing rules of thumb, and develop a better understanding of what has happened and why. Used to look forward, they can help in anticipating future market dynamics – including likely upcoming traps and potential untapped opportunities.

'Strategy is sixty percent fluke and forty percent thought.'
– Michael Drabbe, Member, Managing Board, ABN-AMRO Bank

What's past may be prologue ...
... but first make sure the history makes sense

Take a look at Fig. 3.5. It's one I see frequently at clients, who tell me that something like this accurately reflects their market.

If you translate the story imbedded in this competitive-game map into words, you'll see why I say this is a 'perplexing' diagram. What Fig. 3.5 says is the following: if you want some benefits at a medium price, buy product B. If you want more benefits but at a higher price, buy product C or even product D. But product A: such a deal! Relative to the other alternatives, you pay the most and get the least.

Clearly, if A has any market share, or if its market share is doing anything other than declining rapidly, something is missing from this map. It could be that there are regulatory barriers. It could be that product A has high switching costs, effectively making the total cost for moving to products B, C, and D prohibitively expensive and therefore higher than shown on the chart. It could be that there are information barriers, in which case, if you are any player other than A, you want to broadcast the message about

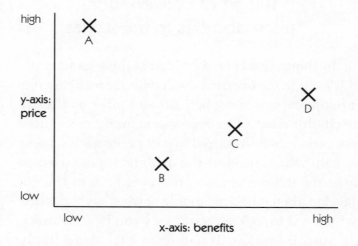

Fig. 3.5   Example of a perplexing competitive-game map.

your product loudly and clearly. Or it could be that you've got the x-axis wrong.

Going back to the Rolex example in Chapter 2, Rolex would be put in the position of product A in Fig. 3.5 if you used an x-axis that only showed performance (accuracy of time keeping, ease and incidence of maintenance). But the real x-axis for Rolex wearers is probably more like the one in Fig. 3.6, as sketched out for me by an English executive in a Dutch company who declared that his Rolex was the best purchase he had made in ten years, explaining that it 'makes me feel great about myself,' a claim that I can't make about my old, beat-up Seiko (but I can make about several suits in my closet). Many people make purchases that hit the hot button of 'makes me feel great' ... even if the item in question isn't a watch.

As the comparison of the competitive-game map in Fig. 3.5 versus the x-axis in Fig. 3.6 shows, if the market data don't support the story indicated by your map, it probably means that there's some assumption you've made that needs to be challenged.

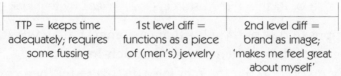

Fig. 3.6 X-Axis for Rolex customers.

Rules of Thumb Save Time ...
But They Also Can Cost Markets

One manager I know, when confronted with a bad decision based on a standard rule of thumb, mumbled something under his breath about cutting off thumbs. A less Draconian approach, perhaps, is to use competitive-game maps to challenge the 'conventional wisdom' prevailing in your organization. Take rules of thumb about what customers want and what they will pay. Before you continue to play by these axioms, it can be useful to see what new or revised competitive-game map assumptions would disprove these rules. Then you can create what I think of as 'what-if maps,' revised competitive-game maps that can be used to see what opportunities or threats could emerge if the new set of assumptions held true.

Rule of thumb #1: 'the market will never pay that much'

This is the rule of thumb that almost sank the Cuisinart food processor, which its inventor, Carl Sontheimer, tried to bring to market in 1973. In fact, when buyers for upscale department stores in the US saw the new device and its $175 retail price, versus blenders that sold for a fraction of that price at the time, some laughed so hard that tears welled up in their eyes – until, that is, *Gourmet* magazine called the device 'indispensable' and explained why. That created new territory on the competitive-game map and Cuisinart sales exploded.

Rule of thumb #2: 'customers will never buy that junk'

The opposite rule of thumb – that customers will never accept a reduced number of benefits for a much lower price – can be equally myopic, as Sontheimer later discovered. When competitor Sunbeam introduced the 'OSKAR,' a stripped-down, pint-sized food processor selling for about $60, Sontheimer ignored it, regarding the new product as a joke. But the OSKAR was based on research that showed that half of the big machines were sitting unused in kitchens across America – and that they were unused because they were seen as too big, too complicated, or too hard to clean. OSKAR therefore created a new space on the competitive-game map between blenders and high-end processors, selling 750,000 units in 1985, and another 1,400,000 the next year. It took several years before Cuisinart admitted the 'gum ball machine' was an important part of the market, though by that time the company was already in deep financial difficulties.

Rule of thumb #3: 'we can control the pricing in our market'

Because all pricing decisions must be made in the context of how you think competitors will adjust their prices in response, adding costs to the competitive-game map is a better way to estimate what competitors will or won't do than relying on old standards. Consider the example in Fig. 3.7, where the check marks show the price/benefit positions of each of five competing products, and the 'X's' below the letters show the cost position of each. In one situation I observed that looked much like this, product D was the market share leader, and product E was the new kid in the market.

As you would have predicted from the map, the entry of product E into the market, which gave more benefits than product D for only a small increment in price, had resulted in significant share losses for product D. The question was whether D should

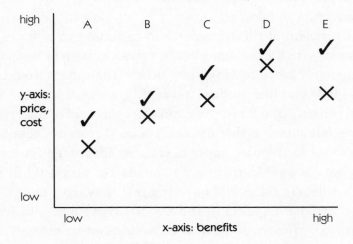

Fig. 3.7 Competitive-game map for Company D's pricing decision. ('✓' indicates price of each product; 'X' beneath indicates the vendor's cost to produce and deliver that product.)

reduce its price to retaliate. I argued against the move as the analysis of costs, as shown in chart, indicated that Company E could respond by dropping its prices such that it would continue to make money (though less than it had been) and D would start losing money. The counter argument was that since D was the market leader, it had to 'teach the upstart a lesson.' The counter argument prevailed. You can imagine the outcome: E dropped its prices, kept its market share and still made some margin while forcing D to lower its prices to a cash-hemorrhaging point. Education had indeed occurred, but the lesson was that E was now the market maker.

Rule of thumb #4: 'we can increase our margins by cutting our costs'

Putting costs on the competitive-game maps can also remind you that if you lower the costs of your product, you need to check to see if you are also moving to the left on the x-axis – that is, reducing the benefits as well. Then, if you have cut benefits as well as costs, you need to test how confident you are that you are still providing a good deal relative to the alternatives, despite the reduction in benefits.

The problem of cutting benefits to customers in order to gain cost savings for the company doesn't go away with fancy marketing language. Take electronic plane tickets. The airlines would have you believe that this product suddenly gives us a new and wonderful benefit – and for free: we can't lose our tickets. But I reckon the real advantage is that the ticket-related costs are about one-tenth those for regular paper tickets, an advantage for the airlines, not for us. Meanwhile, customers get no break on price and lose the confidence of knowing that they have their tickets no matter what happens at the airport. That's a benefit I value highly – even more so now after having observed passengers nearly come to blows with other passengers who had taken their seats or with gate attendants blocking their entry onto planes, either because their e-tickets got lost somewhere in airline cyberspace or because they weren't carrying the exact credit card on which their e-ticket had been billed. Thanks, but I'll be old fashioned and stick with paper.

Seeing into the future …
… of analysis, imagination, and faith

One of the most foolish debates in business is the one between two dueling axioms, 'if it ain't broke, don't fix it' versus 'fix it even if it ain't broke.' The problem with both is that decisions about what to change, why and how require judgment, not proverbs. The acid tests, and the competitive-game maps that illustrate them, help by providing ways to explain past movements in the market and anticipate new ones. Then the task is to apply imagination and faith, key ingredients for jumping from analysis to actions aimed at shaping markets or your position in them.

For example, newspapers in the US complain bitterly about their steady decline in readership. Yet if you denominate the y-axis in time, it becomes clear that the benefits on the x-axis need to be those that encourage people to read their papers. What about:

- Keeping articles short and putting the supplemental materials into additional, short articles for those who want in-depth information (but still in digestible chunks)?

- Investing in reporters and editors who can create interesting, well written, well edited stories?

- Making the layout of the paper more predictable, so reader can find what they're looking for – including the rest of the story they started on page 1 – quickly and easily?

- Using ink that doesn't smear on readers' hands, clothes and furniture?

All of these ideas appear repeatedly in surveys of what newspaper readers in the US want – and all of them are promptly ignored by most newspapers under the reasoning that it makes no

'Put it before them briefly so they will read it, clearly so they will appreciate it, picturesquely so they will remember it and, above all, accurately so they will be guided by its light.'
– Joseph Pulitzer (1847–1911), American journalist and newspaper owner

sense to make additional investments in an old technology because the Internet is killing print. No, the Internet is supplementing print; it's short-sighted publishers who are killing the print-news business by withholding investments that will attract readers, and therefore advertisers.

Or consider dry cleaners. A complete map of all the dry cleaners in my general neighborhood looks something like the one shown in Fig. 3.8.

When I look at this map, I see an abundance of opportunities. One is for makers of spot-removers-in-a-can and home dry-cleaning kits (neither of which may clean as well as an outside establishment could but both of which at least removes the risk of misshapened lapels, missing buttons, torn-out shoulder pads or – my dry cleaners' latest invention – trouser pleats along the outer side seam

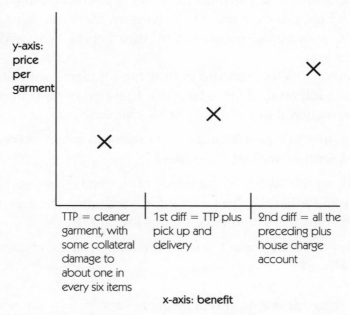

y-axis: price per garment

TTP = cleaner garment, with some collateral damage to about one in every six items	1st diff = TTP plus pick up and delivery	2nd diff = all the preceding plus house charge account

x-axis: **benefit**

Fig. 3.8 My options for choice of a dry cleaners.

of each leg). Another is to change the x-axis (benefits) by making the TTP represent cleaner garments with no or rare collateral damage to the clothing. People who know the dry-cleaning business tell me that such a shift is possible: it's a matter of time and attention by the staff. That sounds to me like the perfect franchising opportunity: a market that needs standards and consistency in implementing them, just as McDonald's has done in fast foods and Marriott in hotels.

Competitive-game maps like the one in Fig. 3.8 and the others in this chapter can provide explanations, open new questions, prompt ideas. As strategy is made in your company, what efforts are in place to ensure that the content of those conversations are around the issues that matter?

• • •

N Brown Group plc is a UK catalogue home-shopping company with a number of catalogue titles, including JD Williams and Ambrose Wilson. Most of the sales are of 'ladies' clothing' to women N Brown politely calls 'mid life.' Revenues in 1997 topped £280 million.

N Brown's manifesto about its business goes this way: 'People differ. An appreciation of this simple fact underpins N Brown's unique approach to home shopping. We refuse to homogenise our customers. We endeavor to know more about them, about their tastes, their expectations of quality and their size specifications. From what we learn we are able to tailor our services ... to satisfy their requirements. This understanding makes us different. It gives N Brown a competitive advantage and drives our business success.'

N Brown's decisions about package delivery provide one example of how the company uses its philosophy to drive business success. Its competitors use independent companies to deliver their parcels. N Brown decided to ship through the UK postal system ... and to use its own people in each local area to deliver packages to customers and pick up returns. The result: easier pick-ups and deliveries for customers plus the opportunity for a person-to-person relationship with a company that would otherwise remain faceless; increased customer loyalty for N Brown plus a lower cost, more flexible system for getting its packages where it wants them to be. These results in turn have contributed to the company's financial record of high after-tax return on sales, growth in revenues, and corresponding love affair with investors on the UK exchange.

Strategy is about action, not words. But for most companies, most of the time, key shifts in strategy emerge out of conversation: about what game to play, why, and how to alter it to your own advantage. Whether your company is a market leader, like N Brown, or a market laggard, you always face the same choice: to make these decisions easily but with little awareness and then hope for the best, or to uncover the driving assumptions and engage in real debate about their likely fit to future conditions. As you consider these two options, you might keep in mind the words of Clint Eastwood in the film *Dirty Harry*, which ran along these lines: 'The question is ... how lucky do you feel?'

The Sins of Organization

When students at Harvard Business School talk about their studies, they often express strong dissatisfaction with the organizational behavior courses, particularly in comparison to the 'real' stuff – strategy, marketing and finance. If you attend a fifth-year reunion, however, the same people frequently espouse a radically different point of view, especially those whose jobs require them to do rather than to advise. Then the emerging consensus is that it's been the 'soft' courses, the same ones that they scoffed at as students, that have provided the greatest utility as they have had to work as part of a team to implement ideas and plans.

It's not surprising why. Despite ubiquitous corporate claims that 'people are our most important asset,' turning such beautiful sentiments into reality requires that two conditions be met: (1) that the people in question possess the skills and judgment to do their jobs well; and (2) that these people are willing to invest effort to do so. This may seem quite obvious, until you observe some organizations – perhaps even your own – committing one or both of the two Deadly Sins of Organization, which may be summarized as follows:

- Sin #4: Banking on turbo-charged employees ... while short-changing the investments needed to build the required skill sets.

- Sin #5: Focusing on workplace sizzle ... but neglecting to provide the motivators that matter.

People are the most difficult part of any workplace equation. Each of us is peculiar in our own unique ways, bringing different levels of ability, standards of judgment, personal hot buttons, and lenses of perception to every event and matter at hand. And each of us is involved in an ongoing saga, which might be entitled, 'My autobiography, starring me.' In consequence, companies cannot operate without the 'soft stuff'; the art of management requires melding a collection of diverse individuals into a coherent and consistent operating force. Many have succeeded, and have been rewarded richly for their efforts. But as generations of new managers have learned, committing either of The Deadly Sins of Organization guarantees that the company's people will be transformed from potential asset into potential liability – sometimes even into the company's most dangerous and intransigent liability.

Turbo-Charged Employees

*Show up on time,
know your words,
don't bump into things.*

– Actor Charlton Heston
on what it takes to do your job well
if you're in front of the camera
in the movie business

Signs when a company touts its people as its key asset...
... but then doesn't invest in accordance with its words

- A competitor consistently seems to have some sort of invisible edge as it executes its strategy; you can feel but you can't duplicate it at your own company.

- Company literature extols the importance of employees. Senior executives, however, spend little time thinking about or engaging in issues related to building the capabilities of the company's people, thereby reflecting the widely held corporate belief that such issues are of low status and importance relative to the big strategic decisions that 'real managers' make.

- Top executives, as well as the savvy up-and-comers, see the Human Resources department as a kind of in-house employment and compliance agency. HR staff members return the compliment by focusing exclusively on process, procedures, protocols, and prepackaged programs, and on putting as many rules and regulations as they can into company manuals.

- Much of the workforce seems to be afflicted with PBD – passive blindness disease; that is, people don't do more than the minimum because they either don't know how to spot the opportunities to make such extra efforts or don't know how to implement them effectively.

- People who spend significant time coaching and developing others are seen as managerial losers: 'too soft' to make the 'really tough' decisions.

- Despite formal policies and proclamations to the contrary, review of hiring and promotion patterns shows no correlation or even an inverse relationship between hands-on efforts to develop internal capabilities and career advancement.

- Employees are required to attend a whole series of slickly packaged training programs which, in the main, they find to be boring, irrelevant, insulting, or some mix of the three. Despite such assessments, the programs aren't changed, either because the participants aren't asked for their comments or, if asked, their evaluations are disregarded as immaterial or otherwise 'misinformed.'

- The company's underlying approach to empowerment can be summarized in three words: 'Poof ... you're empowered!' (For British, Australian and other non-American readers, substitute 'bingo' for 'poof' in the preceding.) Despite the brevity incantation, little difference is evident in what the people so empowered actually do.

You may not know how to define it, and you may not know it right away, but you can generally sense when you're dealing with an enterprise where the employees themselves have become a competitive advantage. In some places, you sense it the minute you cross the threshold. In others, it takes longer for you to sense this invisible edge, but bit by bit you begin to see that there is something special about the way the people interact with each other, their work, their customers, and their suppliers. In the same way, the reverse also becomes apparent. Then, even companies that seem comparable on paper, show out in action, falling further and further behind their competitors.

A small example of the comparison is the brunch my husband and I almost had at a luxurious and famous Boston restaurant I'll call The Bostonia. While the restaurant was less than a third full, no one acknowledged our presence as we waited to be seated, even though three wait staff, none of whom appeared to be otherwise occupied, stood within six feet of us. After a bit, we decamped and set off for the Boston branch of the Canadian Four Seasons hotel chain. Here our experience was just the opposite. While the restaurant was packed, we weren't at the doorway for more than 30 seconds before a young man in a white jacket greeted us, checked the reservations book, surveyed the room, and led us to a table.

'Ability will never catch up with demand for it.'
– Malcolm S. Forbes (1919–1990)

There's nothing unusual about this story, except for one detail: the dress code for the staff. As we enjoyed our meal, I noticed that the waitresses were all attired in print silk dresses; the restaurant managers, in grey business suits. And our young man in the white jacket? He was among an army of similarly garbed colleagues, all of whom were very busy … pouring water, refilling coffee cups, and clearing tables. Our maitre d' was an 'associate server' – or what used to be called a busboy.

Given that The Four Seasons, Boston has a reputation for this kind of extra effort, it probably won't surprise you that the initiative of this employee multiplied by similar initiatives taken every day by other staff members adds to the hotel's bottom line. In the actual case, though, when the Boston Four Seasons opened for business in 1986, it faced serious structural barriers: deeply entrenched competitors with fabulous reputations and seemingly unassailable advantages in location, physical plant and prestige. These difficulties notwithstanding, ten years later, the Four Seasons Boston was the only five-diamond hotel in New England, as rated by the American Automobile Association. Its dinner restaurant, the Aujourd'hui, was the only five-diamond restaurant in Massachusetts. And, with an occupancy rate of well over 80 percent – meaning that it was essentially sold out every night – the hotel had the highest occupancy in Boston and one of the highest in the entire country.

Many managers, convinced by stories like these, say they subscribe to the belief that what their employees do everyday can create competitive advantage. Nonetheless, few actually seem to be able to turn the theory into results. Why? Well, for one thing, many managers severely underestimate the number and impact of unsupervised (and unsupervisable) decisions that every person in the organization makes every day. And for another, many invest far too little in building what I call the 'judgment reservoir' of the organization – the shared understanding of what to do and how to do it.

Which brings us back to the OODA Loop introduced in Chapters 2 and 3. The OODA Loop, as you might recall, refers to USAF pilot John R. Boyd's insight that superior air-attack strategies start with superior ability to go through the constant cycle of observation, orientation, decision, and action (the O, O, D, and A of the OODA Loop) quickly and well. In those chapters, I used the OODA Loop to look at and test the big strategy decisions. In this one, I apply the OODA Loop to smaller decisions, the ones that all employees make every day and that provide the basis for real learning at all levels in an organization.

My reason for doing so is simple: these small, everyday decisions are the ones that can enhance a mediocre strategy – and effectively kill others that, at least on paper, look great. Companies whose workforces provide an invisible edge help their employees become more aware of the choice points they encounter and more competent about the decisions they make in response to each. Otherwise, and no matter how motivated the employees are (the topic of the next chapter), you run the risk of a defective OODA Loop: observe incompletely, orient and decide incorrectly, act ineffectively. Then, though each person still faces a continuous stream of choice points each day, the resulting decisions contribute far less to the company's position than was possible – and less than the comparable decisions at a competitor, as happened at the Bostonia versus the Four Seasons.

Part one
A hundred unsupervised decisions a day...
... per employee

How can companies help their people to use the OODA Loop well? The starting point is this trio of realities about employee decision-making:

1   *Every* employee makes on the order of a hundred decisions per day.

2   The cumulative effect of these decisions is substantial, enough to either enhance or negate the big strategic decisions that set the overall direction for an organization.

3   Managers can neither fully supervise nor completely control these decisions and actions; and, worse, the more managers try to eliminate decisions from their subordinates' jobs, the further they get from the invisible edge held by enterprises like the Four Seasons Boston.

But here's the thing. While these statements may sound like gross exaggerations, they are, if anything, substantial understatments. A closer look at the three shows why.

Assertion #1: a hundred decisions a day ...
... more or less

The first thing people usually question is the arithmetic. A hundred decisions per day for anyone is ludicrous, they say; hard to believe for even the CEO of an organization and preposterous for people lower down in the hierarchy (or, for those organizations that claim that they have no hierarchy, read: 'for those who are more junior and/or are paid less than the senior executives'). That said, both data and logic are on my side.

Let's start with the easy part – what CEOs do. Here the academic literature provides great data. Perhaps the most famous of these is the 'shadowing' study in which Henry Mintzberg, Bronfman Professor of Management at McGill University in Montréal, dogged the footsteps of the chief executive officers of five large organizations for a week each, and two similar studies, one by Choron on the CEOs of smaller companies and the other by Guest on 56 foremen. All three researchers found that their subjects were constantly faced with a wide range of activities – anywhere from an average of 77 per day to 583. Each of these activities in turn involved an associated set of decisions – either to wait and do nothing for the moment, or to select and implement an action.

'Big things and little things are my job. Middle-level arrangements can be delegated.'
– Konosuke Matsushita (1894–1989)

Perhaps you're not surprised by these findings. After all, the image most of us have of managers – from CEOs to front-line supervisors – is of busy people making many (important) decisions. Or consider Dan Hole. He's a billboard painter. Every several weeks he gets an original ad from Leo Barnett, the advertising agency for Marlboro cigarettes. Hole's job is take the artwork provided by Leo Barnett and then reproduce it in paint on plywood on a gigantic scale – say, 60 feet by 35 feet or so. Though he makes the image bigger, he otherwise sticks with the instructions from the agency. Some people might regard Hole as a strictly paint-by-the-numbers kind of guy with few work decisions that haven't already been made for him. But that's not how he sees it. Instead, Hole describes his job as 'making hundreds of decisions constantly ... what tone, how sharp, how soft, how subtle, how overt.' Though the overall framework has been provided, he faces endless smaller choices about interpretation, choices that taken together make a substantial difference in the final product.

Or, finally, let's go back to the busboy at the Four Seasons. In the several moments that his job and our search for breakfast intersected, he had any number of options. First, he could have ignored us, on the understanding that attending to people at the maitre d's podium was 'not his job,' just as the wait staff at The Bostonia did. But he also had several other options, any one of which would have satisfied us as prospective customers. For example, he could have: come by and told us that he would let a manager know that we were waiting; smiled at us and notified a manager that new customers had appeared; or even smiled and nodded at us, and done nothing more. And, all told, this entire romp through the OODA Loop – from observation to action, occupied, at most, only several minutes of his eight-hour shift.

But clearly, these weren't his only decisions for the day. A busboy (or 'associate server' as people in this role are called at the Four Seasons) faces a constant stream of choice points over the course of every shift: when to clear the dishes (especially if one person is still eating and the others appear to have finished their meals), whether to pour more water (especially if the people at the table seem deep in conversation), whether to attend to a diner trying to flag a waiter and then to transmit the request to the appropriate person (even if doing so isn't technically part of the associate server's job).

A few thought experiments also suggest that it's not just serv-ice organizations like hotels, restaurants, hospitals or airlines where employees make so many decisions each day. People who work in research laboratories, component-fabrication plants, steel mills, software firms, order-fulfillment telephone rooms, shop floors, accounting firms, and truck-factory assembly lines also face a continuous flow of decisions. Though some of these are diffi-cult to document, they're still decisions: whether to offer an idea or withhold it; call attention to a small defect in a product or let it ride down the line; really pay attention to a customer or give the closest standard answer to a non-standard inquiry. Though many times such choice points are virtually invisible, make no mistake: if there's more than one path that can be taken, a decision has been made (even if you can't see it).

That means that all employees are making decisions, regard-less of management's point of view about the matter. In many organizations therefore the question of the moment is not whether the employees should be given powers they already have, but whether they know how to go though Boyd's OODA Loop faster and more effectively than their counterparts at competing firms.

Assertion #2: a hundred decisions a day ...
... per employee × every employee

But if my numbers are correct, I am often told, then it's my abil-ity to do my sums that is lacking. Okay, the argument goes, maybe it is true that a lot of people are making a lot of little decisions. But in terms of impact, the sum of a bunch of tiny decisions is still a small number, especially relative to the big, strategic deci-sions that determine the direction of an entire organization.

This is incorrect. Of course the big decisions about organiza-tional direction count. But this is not an 'either/or' situation. The small ones add up too, and the cumulative effect of these non-strategic decisions can be quite substantial. The difficulty is that the connection between small decisions made and overall results achieved is exceedingly difficult to see, much less to verify with precision. As a result, calculating the exact monetary impact of the everyday decisions on an organization's bottom line is just about impossible.

For example, consider the reaction of a woman, now the executive vice president of a midsize company, who went to a Brooks Brothers store to buy a present for her beau. As she tells the story, when she found the correct department, she also encountered a gaggle of salespeople, all of whom ignored her for twenty minutes while one of three waited on the only other customer present, an older woman with the air of inherited money. This is how she described the event – several decades after the fact:

> *The brain is a wonderful organ. It starts the moment you get up in the morning and does not stop until you get to the office.'*
> – Robert Frost (1874–1963), American poet

> *I didn't mind the waiting, but I was really angry about how I was treated. While I was waiting, none of the sales staff made eye contact with me or acknowledged my presence in any way. Maybe the other two were busy with another task – it didn't look that way but you never know. But the third fellow just looked through me, like I wasn't there. He didn't say, 'I'll be with you in a while' or 'This will take a few minutes more. Why don't you look around?' Not even a nod to show that he knew I was there. And when he finally did wait on me, he never apologized for the delay.* **He made me feel like a nobody. I made my purchase, but I have never set foot in any of their stores again and I never will.**

With her furs and perfectly coifed hair, the older woman may have been the very image of the kind of customer Brooks Brothers wanted to attract. Indeed, at the time of the interaction in question, my friend was an impecunious graduate student. But she also then represented, by her own calculation, perhaps 60 years of future revenues to the famous clothing-store chain (especially since today, having done better financially than she had ever dreamed, she reckons she could buy most of the contents of a Brooks Brothers store in one outing, and still have a nice nest egg left over). The cost to the company, therefore, was real but invisible. My friend never complained. She just never came back.

For some senior executives, though, there is no doubt about the impact, positive and negative, of the 'daily hundred' made by all employees in an organization. Jan Carlzon, former CEO of Scandinavian Airlines, is one of these managers. Without question, Carlzon's turnaround of SAS was due in part to the big strategic decisions – about aircraft, routes, schedules, costs, and hubs. But by Carlzon's figuring, it was also due to the 136,986 – plus or minus – decisions made by the company's front-line employees each day.

Here's the math: Carlzon calculated that in 1981, when he took on the role of CEO, SAS served 10 million customers annually and that each of these customers in turn spent 15 seconds, on average, with each of the five SAS employees with whom they came into contact. The result, as Carlzon put it, was that 'SAS is "created" 50 million times a year, 15 seconds at a time. These 50 million 'moments of truth' … ultimately decide whether SAS will succeed or fail as a company.' Though he can't put an exact bottom-line number on it, Carlzon clearly understands that many small decisions made by many people every day do hit the bottom line – positively or negatively. If you've never thought about the impact of all these small decisions in your company, chances are that your firm falls into the second category.

Assertion #3: a hundred decisions a day …
… with no means of full managerial control

It's here, at the third of my three assertions about employee decision-making, that I usually run into the strongest resistance. That's because I claim that the daily hundred, though potentially of huge importance, are impossible either to supervise directly or to control completely. My reason for this claim has to do with 'discretion'; that is, the times when each person exercises judgment without direct supervision.

A provocative thinker on this topic is Elliott Jaques, a psychoanalyst and business strategist who bases his conclusions on his work with a diverse group of organizations, including the United States Army, the Church of England, and CRA, the mining company that is one of the largest corporations in Australia. Jaques argues that all employees make decisions all the time and that all decisions involve discretion and judgment. The difference between the decisions taken by an entry-level employee and those taken by a top executive, in his view, lies in the 'time-span' of the judgment involved, which he defines as: 'the maximum time during which the manager must rely upon the discretion of his subordinate and the subordinate works on his own.'

Let's go back to airline employees, those working at SAS or any other carrier. For a gate agent, the biggest choices might revolve around whether to upgrade a ticket, hold a plane at the gate, or refuse to board a drunken passenger – or, more routinely, whether to be helpful to a customer who is in a muddle or needs to make some alternate arrangements, versus doing only the minimum required. Going through the OODA Loop for these decisions takes just moments, although the impact of the resulting actions (or nonactions) on individual customers can extend well into the future – just as the busboy's decision did for me.

In contrast, the time span for the CEO's decisions from inception to implementation can be years, and the net impact of each can touch millions of potential customers for decades. These decisions might include hub design and route selection, aircraft purchase, and personnel policy. Nevertheless, and despite the difference in the nature of their choices, both the gate agent and the CEO are constantly exercising judg-

'You can duplicate airplanes. You can duplicate gate facilities. You can duplicate all the hard things, the tangible things you can put your hands on. But it's the intangibles that determine success. They're the hardest to duplicate, if you can do it at all. We've got the right intangibles.'
– Herb Kelleher, CEO, Southwest Airlines

ment and using their discretion as they make their decisions. Or as Jaques argues, discretion and judgment are part of every job, even though the nature of the choices varies by the level within the organizational hierarchy.

And therein lies the rub. For some managers, the idea that employees exercise discretion across so many decisions is unpleasant and unsettling. A common response is to clamp down, in hopes that more rules, more procedures and more supervision (and today, electronic supervision) will result in fewer opportunities for each person to exercise judgment. There are two problems with this approach. One is that it just isn't possible to script and otherwise control a job so completely that people don't have to use their own judgment at least to some extent. The other is that attempts for total control can alienate a workforce so completely as to just about guarantee that only the minimum, and nothing but the minimum, will be produced.

Consider a job with among the least discretion of any: being a 'tutti' player in a symphony orchestra. Few jobs have less; the score has already been written and selected, you never get to play solo, and then the conductor decides on virtually every aspect of interpretation. And for this reason, it's tempting to imagine that the conductor can control all 100 or so players and how they play with a mere wave of the baton. In fact, when I was in business school, we were shown a film of a conductor masterfully leading a performance of Ravel's 'Bolero,' a wonderfully ego-inflating metaphor for what we – future managers of the world – were going to do in our companies. But the truth is that even orchestra conductors don't have complete control, as a player from the Boston Symphony Orchestra explained to me over lunch one day:

> *A great conductor can get you to do what he needs with the minimum gesture but the maximum respect. He lets you know what he expects from you and then he uses the baton to acknowledge that he knows you can do it. He balances the systems within the orchestra and sets the broad picture*

and then lets you use your discretion for the rest. The more standard conductor, on the other hand, micromanages to the point that individuals can't play or are so angry they don't want to.

And that's precisely the point. Perfect control is impossible; and even if it were possible, the best it could ever achieve is compliance with standards which, in today's competitive environments, is hardly ever enough.

Of course, there is another alternative – what is commonly called 'empowerment' (and what used to be called 'delegation'). But people don't find that they suddenly know what to do and how to do it just because someone taps them lightly with a sword on either shoulder, declares them to be empowered, and urges them to venture forth and make great decisions. Rather, even when the motivation level within the workforce is extremely high, investment – of both time and money – is required to build and deepen the 'judgment reservoir' within the organization.

> *'In our scheme, we do not ask the initiative of our men. All we want of them is to obey the orders we give them, do what we say, and do it quick.'*
> – Frederick Winslow Taylor (1856–1917), business efficiency guru

Part two
Investing in the judgment reservoir...
... and back to Boyd's 'OODA Loop'

Across town from the Four Seasons sits an unlikely comparison, Beth Israel Hospital, a Harvard affiliated teaching hospital known throughout Boston as the BI. As with the Four Seasons, countless publications have rated the BI as one of the best in its industry – including *Business Week*, *Health Forum Journal*, and *The Best Hospitals in America*.

Of the comments from such publications, one of my favorites comes from Ron Zemke's *The Service Edge*. Having named the BI as one of the 101 best service organizations in the US in any industry (and one of only three hospitals – and the only hospital in Boston – to make the list), Zemke makes this observation: 'When you ask Boston doctors to name the best hospital in town, chances are they'll say Massachusetts General.... But a funny thing happens when you rephrase the question and ask them where they would go for treatment if they or someone in their family had to be hospitalized. Then the answer you're likely to get is Beth Israel Hospital.'

Why has the BI gotten such rave reviews? All the Harvard teaching hospitals, the BI and the MGH included, receive high marks for the technical aspects of the medical care they provide and the research they conduct; that's close to the tickets-to-play for their segment of the health care market. The BI's invisible edge, as at the Boston Four Seasons, has arisen from the way the people who work there – doctors, nurses, food servers, administrators, house keepers, guards, phlebotomists, and so on – use their hundred decisions a day to *care* for patients and their families as well as to cure them.

Which brings us to the more interesting question. Holding the matter of motivation for the next chapter, how is it that the people in places like the Four Seasons and BI know what to do in order to create such an invisible edge? I think the answer lies in Boyd's OODA Loop – even though most of the people in these organizations probably wouldn't frame their approach this way (in part, because they may never have heard of Boyd or his loop). More specifically, I think it lies in how the employees in these organizations are trained implicitly to go through each of these four steps of the Loop:

- *Observation:* search actively to see what's happening at present, as well as to understand the consequence of previous actions;

- *Orientation:* place oneself within the evolving situation and associated time constraints, and generate options (including doing nothing);

- *Decision:* mentally 'run the camera forward' on each of the options to forecast likely results and then select one; and

• *Action:* take the selected action in timely fashion – and then observe the actual consequences (back to the observation step).

The rest of this chapter describes the Four Seasons and BI case studies in a bit more depth – how I got to know both enterprises, and what I've learned about the investments each has made in building workforces capable of making great decisions – consistently and at all levels.

The two Boston case studies: glitz and guts

I chose the Four Seasons, Boston and the BI as the case studies for this chapter for three reasons. First, they've been demonstrated leaders in building the judgment reservoirs of their respective organizations. Second, despite surface similarities (beds, meals, service), they represent distinctly different competitive environments, with the BI having far fewer degrees of freedom in almost every element of a business strategy – setting prices, deciding which services and products to offer, ability to collect fees for services already delivered. And third, I had direct access to the data – several hours' worth in the case of the Four Seasons, and several hundred hours' worth in the case of the BI – along with permission to publish the findings in raw form and with attribution.

For the Four Seasons, the case study came as a direct consequence of my brunch. Fascinated by how and why the busboy made his decision to pay attention to us, I called Robin Brown, the British ex-pat manager of the Boston Four Seasons, told him the story, and proposed a deal: I would take him to breakfast at, naturally, The Bostonia, if he would explain to me what he was trying to do at the Four Seasons, and how he was going about it.

> 'Never tell people how to do things. Tell them what you want them to achieve and they will surprise you with their ingenuity.'
> – George Smith Patton Jr. (1885-1945), World War II General, US Army

Robin took me up on my offer and provided me with thought-ful and engaging answers that are described later in this chapter rather than canned corporate responses. (You know the oppo-site. You ask a question, and you get preprogrammed answer #56, the closest one to the question you asked – but not in fact the precise answer to your exact question.)

For the BI, on the other hand, the example used in this chap-ter is based on a research project I supervised over the course of several months using Mintzberg's 'shadowing' methodology. The primary researcher was Elizabeth Glaser who, as she was com-pleting a year of post-MBA work as a Harmon Fellow, found herself stymied. The problem: her research topic was excellent customer service in the financial services industry – but every time she looked closely at a bank that had a great reputation, she found terrific marketing, awesome PR and ... really crummy serv-ice.

When Elizabeth called me for ideas, I suggested some other banks and what I considered a truly odd idea, given her industry focus: the BI. My rationale was simple, since it was based on only one fact – when my husband had knee surgery there, neither of us could think of a single thing to complain about (even though I can – and routinely, do – complain about everything).

'If you haven't anything nice to say about anybody, come sit next to me.'
– Alice Roosevelt Longworth (1884–1980), daughter of Theodore Roosevelt, 26th president of the United States

Subsequently, Elizabeth and I met with Mitchell Rabkin, the BI's physician-CEO, who gave us permission for unre-stricted access to the hospital, with Elizabeth as the pri-mary researcher. Working with Robert Eccles, a professor at Harvard Business School, we designed the study using the Mintzberg approach. That put Elizabeth on a two-month journey during which she shadowed 23 BI-ers – among them doctors (chiefs of service to residents, the new doctors who had come to the BI for their post-gradu-ate training), food servers, nurses, nurse managers, house-keepers, and others – for at least one work shift each. We also conducted 48 in-depth interviews at the BI, and reviewed a pile of findings from previous surveys of people who had been patients at both the BI and other area hospitals. Based on her experience with financial institutions, Elizabeth began the study with the bias that the BI couldn't possibly be as good as its reputation. She came away from the research convinced of quite the opposite.

These two case studies confirm characteristics that I've seen repeatedly in other places where people at all levels know what to do and how to do it. Both start with an explicit commitment; at the Boston Four Seasons it's for everyone to do what Robin Brown calls 'taking a step forward' – figuring out what can be done next that improve the guest's experience and the hotel's performance – just as the busboy did during our Sunday-brunch encounter. At the BI, it's for everyone to contribute to delivering what one physician describes as 'medicine with grace'; the best combination of technical care and human caring. And both go about realizing their goals in very similar ways:

1   They view hiring decisions as *asset* decisions, and accordingly put significant investment, especially of time, into making certain they hire the right people.

2   They pay close attention to removing organizational obstacles to individual performance, particularly in how they structure and describe key jobs.

3   They invest constantly, consistently and personally in active, real-time coaching; that's the managerial ingredient that helps people move from core tasks to the extras that create an invisible edge.

4   Without question and all rhetoric aside, the overall definition of 'the right thing' starts at the top – with the top executives' core beliefs, behaviors, and selection of direct reports.

These four characteristics may all seem quite obvious. But as you read through the brief descriptions of how the Boston Four Seasons and the BI execute against them, ask yourself a set of simple questions: how much time and attention do the people in your organization invest in each of these areas?

1. 'We don't compromise on people': who invests the time to get the right staff?

Every company has to hire people; even 'virtual companies' have to select the people who will be part of their team. But many companies delegate this task to their HR staff, with little investment from people in the rest of the organization. How much investment in finding the right people does your organization make, and who makes it?

At the Boston Four Seasons, I didn't even have to ask this question to get the answer. Rather, when I asked about the busboy, Robin Brown responded by talking about the hiring process:

*First you have to understand how we hire. We typically give six to eight interviews per candidate, and I or the Assistant General Manager see every candidate that has a reasonable chance of being hired, at least for the final interview. We do **not** use a format of set questions. We also do **not** use psychological tests, like some other places. That would just defeat the purpose. What we're looking for is the kind of person the candidate is.*

*When I interview, I look at everything: how they sit as they wait for the interview, what they are reading, as well as what happens in the interview. I listen to what they say and their body language. Usually, my judgment is the same as the people who have seen the candidate before me, but not always, and then I'll veto a hire. I look especially hard when I know that we are one person short on a complement of staff; for example, when we have seven wait staff and need eight. Then, if the candidate is marginal, I'll exercise my veto, first because it's the right decision, but also to send a message: **we don't compromise on people.***

'This woman is headstrong, obstinate and dangerously self-opinionated.'
– 1948 report from an HR officer, rejecting Margaret Thatcher for a job at ICI

The same finding was evident at the BI. One middle manager told Glaser: 'I couldn't believe how seriously they took the interviewing process. When I came here, I interviewed with thirteen people, from the medical director to the unit coordinator [a clerical position].' A nurse manager sounded a similar theme: 'I look for values in the people I hire. I try and get a sense of the person. The kinds of questions that I ask include those which get at values through situational questions. If the person answers the question with a remark about some technical aspect of care, then they are a very different person than one who will tell you a personal story about some aspect of care. I don't think any of my staff asks this question in the same way, but I suspect that as they talk to people, they try to figure out the same things.'

Though hiring the right people isn't the whole answer to building a judgment reservoir, it clearly does make all the other required tasks significantly easier. Nonetheless, in many companies, hiring is regarded as requiring input only from the direct supervisor and the HR department, thereby yielding a limited view of a candidate's potential fit with the organization and its goals. In others, it's viewed as something akin to purchasing relatively undifferentiated widgets; a low status task that merits little managerial investment. Yet all chefs worth their salt know that a great recipe made with poor ingredients produces, at best, only a mediocre meal. If your mission statement extols the company's people as 'our most important asset,' take a second look at the actual process used in the last several hires – and especially at who spent time with the candidates, and how these people made their hiring decisions. Then ask yourself, was enough time spent by the right people to arrive at the hiring decisions your organization needs?

'Few great men could pass Personnel.' – Paul Goodman (1911–1972)

2. 'It's the nurses!': how easy is it for people to do their jobs well?

When Mitch Rabkin was appointed president of the Beth Israel Hospital in 1966, he was 36 years old, and the biggest group he had ever managed was an endocrinology lab at the Massachu-setts General Hospital. As he began assessing his new surround-ings shortly after his arrival at the BI, he quickly came to the conclusion that the quality of nursing care was among the issues he had to address. So far there's nothing out of the ordinary about this perception; in private, many hospital CEOs worry about the quality of care being provided by the nurses in their institutions.

But what Rabkin did next was quite unusual, especially among physicians and especially in the 1960s. He came to the realization that nursing care is as important to patient outcomes as physi-cian care, and decided to recruit a new head of nursing who would be capable of rethinking what nurses did and how they did it. He got exactly what he was looking for (and possibly more) in Joyce Clifford, previously the top nurse at two other large hospital sys-tems, who joined the BI and subsequently revolutionized hospi-tal care by revolutionizing nursing.

The Clifford revolution started with the concept of 'primary nursing,' in which each patient is assigned to a primary nurse who coordinates and is accountable for all nursing care while the patient is in the hospital. These nurses, in turn, report to Nurse Managers who, in effect, are the general managers of their units. If you have ever been a patient in an acute-care hospital, you will immediately appreciate the benefits of such an arrangement; your care is still mostly provided by nurses, but with the BI approach you and your family have a person to talk to who knows your case intimately and can help you navigate through the healthcare system.

Others have noticed these benefits as well, and today the BI's model for primary nursing is recognized worldwide as a superior way to deliver high-quality hospital care. Though the process of restructuring and redesign continues at the BI, the core principle remains constant: structure jobs to make the most of the abilities and judgment of the incumbents. That way you get more from your people – and your people get more from their jobs.

But not all jobs need to be restructured, redefined, or reengineered. Sometimes the most helpful thing management can do is simply to take the guesswork out of understanding how to do the core tasks at hand well. That's what Brown and his colleagues did at the Boston Four Seasons, by describing each job in terms of the seventy or so components that comprise baseline performance. For example, for Bell Attendants (whom the politically incorrect among us would call 'bell boys'), the description begins with 'starting your shift,' which is divided into five activities – checking out keys; obtaining a uniform; signing in; reviewing return-guest and VIP lists; and debriefing with the concierge – and each of these in turn is described in a fair amount of detail.

In some settings, job descriptions like these would be used in an attempt to keep employees from thinking. At the Four Seasons, the purpose is just the opposite. If you don't have to spend your time figuring out what it is you need to do to get the core tasks right, you have more time to figure out, in Robin Brown's terms, how to go beyond these minimums and 'take a step forward.'

'High expectations are the key to everything.' – Sam Walton (1918–1992), founder of the Wal-Mart retail empire

Now think about your own organization. How much effort is put into making it easier for employees to do their jobs well and then do more than the minimum? Conversely, do you have a good sense of the barriers that keep people from contributing all that they could – and would like to?

3. 'Subordinates always observe those above them anyway ...': who does the coaching, how much, when, and how?

If I had to pick one thing that is most distinctive about the people in places like the Four Seasons and the BI, though, it wouldn't be the time committed to hiring, or even the time invested in job design and description; it would be the time committed to coaching – real-time and all the time.

Robin Brown was clear on the importance of coaching, and how it produces on-the-job learning that contributes directly to the hotel's performance:

> *We coach constantly. We have a formal coaching program, where more senior people are assigned to new people and to "rewind the tape" – review what just happened, see if there was a better option and why. But everyone's expected to rewind the tape and to coach; that's how we manage ourselves ...*
>
> *Look, here's something that just happened. You know, a hotel can go to hell in two weeks. A few days ago, one of our managers saw some cigarette butts in the driveway toward the entry, so he picked up the butts and brought them to the head doorman. When the doorman started to take the butts, though, the manager said, "No, I can throw them away, that's not the problem. The problem is how this entry area is beginning to look. So we need to bring this up to the staff; shall I or will you?"*
>
> *Now, given that conversation, I know that the head doorman will bring the issue up with his staff, and we'll go on from there. The next day there'll be some positive reinforcement. This is a tough environment but it's also supportive. We don't hold back when there's a problem; we're in your face about it. But then we joke or clap you on the back; we want to make sure everyone's okay.*

At the BI, Glaser observed the same kind of passion for coaching, at all levels within the hospital.

- A nutrition supervisor gives her employees the following pep talk every day before they hit the floors: 'All right, now remember what you are supposed to do out there. Knock on the door, smile, say hello, and put down the tray.' One of the food servers later confides that the short speech had nothing to do with Glaser's presence; 'she [the supervisor] always gives us a pep talk.'

- A housekeeping supervisor describes his job: 'I talk to them about the importance of saying hello when they go in the room. I think that it's important. They don't need to speak English just to be nice, polite and say hello.' A manager of the hospital's laundry services shares a similar philosophy: 'I spend a lot of time trying to get the people in the laundry to understand that what they do is patient care too.'

- A nurse manager explains why she puts so much emphasis on coaching: 'I believe there is a relationship between happy employees and satisfied patients. I learned a lot about this behavior from my mother. I have also learned a lot about this from my boss.'

- William Silen, then the Surgeon-in-Chief, declares emphatically that taking time to make sure patients and their families understand what is happening and why is part of being a good surgeon. 'At the Beth Israel, being concerned with the patient isn't regarded as being soft,' he explains. 'Other hospitals would say that isn't sufficiently macho, but you don't do well here if you are abrupt with patients.' In private, the surgical residents confide that Dr Silen is as good as his word.

So perhaps it's not a surprise that Nurse-in-Chief Clifford says the BI has 'a socialization process, not an orientation process.' Or that Rabkin takes the following view: 'We try to make all our staff in the hospital aware that they are role models, that you are what you do … This attitude has to go everywhere, it's not just teaching them the *content* of medicine, it's teaching them *how* to be doctors, and it's the same with our managers. Subordinates always observe those above them anyway, so we try to use the opportunity consciously.'

But if the people in your organization are observing the people above them and around them, *what*, exactly, are they observing?

Is there enough coaching to teach them how to go through the OODA Loop faster and more effectively than they could before – and faster and more effectively than their counterparts at competing organizations? Or are they modeling behaviors that will keep you stuck somewhere between the middle and the back of the pack?

4. 'You know, it all starts at the top': what messages do your behaviors (and your hires) send?

Shortly after Rabkin settled in his new office as President of the BI, he was visited by Max Feldberg, a generous contributor to the hospital, who proposed a little stroll through the facilities. Stopping at one patient floor, he suggested that they pick up every other piece of litter they happened to see. Next, Feldberg took Rabkin to another patient floor, where they wandered around and chatted, but didn't pick up any debris. Then he directed Rabkin back to the two floors. On the first one, most of the remaining litter was now gone; the second was as messy as it had been before. At which point Feldberg looked at Rabkin and said, 'Never think you're so fancy that you can't pick up the trash. If you don't do it, why should anybody else?' Today, decades later, if you go to the BI you will see many BI-ers stooping to pick up litter, almost subconsciously, as they make their way around the campus. As one of the chiefs of service (and one of the most senior doctors in the hospital), explained 'Mitch picks up paper from the floor, so I do too.'

In fact, at both the Boston Four Seasons and BI one sees CEOs who have been shaped by their bosses, and who similarly then shape the rest of the people in their organizations. When Robin Brown describes his boss, Four Seasons founder Isadore Sharp, you can hear echoes of the influence:

'You do not lead by hitting people over the head – that's assault, not leadership.'
– Dwight David Eisenhower (1890–1969), World War II general and 34th president of the United States

When Izzy comes to visit, he doesn't spend more than five minutes in my office. Typically, he'll go to the men's locker room first, to see if it's clean and how the morale is. When he talks to me and to the other people around here, he wants to know how people are feeling, what the tone of the place is. When he's here, we rarely talk about budgets – he'll do that by phone with me. Izzy knows what he wants and what he wants these places to be. So when I interview, I say to myself, "Is this the kind of person Izzy would like? Is this the kind of person I would like? Is this the kind of person our customers would like?"

But the person who, I think, put it best was Brown's assistant, Jeannine Roy who, during a phone conversation with me, lowered her voice and confided, 'You know, it all starts at the top. Mr Brown says if you ask someone to do something, you should be willing to do it too. He does that, so we do too.'

Which leads to the final questions: whatever your position, what does your behavior tell other people about what to do and how to do it in your organization? And what about the behavior of the people who report directly to you. This is walking the talk for real – not just for motivational purposes, but also for modeling purposes. After all, empowerment is just an empty word if employees don't understand what's involved in 'taking a step forward' and how to do it.

• • •

Somewhere between the Four Seasons and the BI, sits Durgin-Park, a family style restaurant housed in a revolutionary-war era building and famous for its roast beef, Indian pudding, and rude waitresses.

These waitresses are a bit like your maiden aunt Agatha, who used to teach third grade and still takes no guff from anyone, but saltier ('You want some water? Go get your own [expletive deleted] water!'). Once I had dinner there with a group of three friends, one of whom, determined to be unhappy, had decided to converse sparsely, and then only in a small voice and short, morose sentences. That was fine, because we were seated at a long plank table with other diners and soon everyone was talking and laughing with everyone else – except for Stacey, who remained silent and glum.

All of us ordered roast beef and then the Indian pudding and ate it all; Stacey ordered the turkey platter and then strawberry shortcake, and ate about two bites of each. When the waitress, who I'll call Edna, came around to clear the table of the remains of both our dinners and our desserts, Stacey asked for a doggy bag. I think perhaps that at that point Edna had had quite enough. For without a moment's hesitation, she whipped out a bag from a pocket in her apron, picked up Stacey's dinner platter, and let everything – turkey, stuffing, gravy, peas, and cranberry sauce – glide ever so slowly into the bag. Then she put down that plate, picked up Stacey's dessert plate, and even more slowly and deliberately – slid the strawberry shortcake into the mix, rolled the top of bag closed, smacked it down in front of Stacey, and then walked away, muttering to herself. After a collective gasp, everyone at the table (except for Stacey, of course) burst out in uncontrolled laughter.

When you think about it, Edna's performance was effective because she worked in a setting that was renowned for its rudeness and she knew how to tread the line between what customers would perceive as charming irascibility – versus what they would see as unacceptable nastiness. In fact, Durgin-Park's ambiance and reputation are the result of an army of Ednas making these kinds of decisions hundreds of times a day, year in and year out. Yet despite its justly deserved fame, Durgin-Park faces a challenge: how to find replacements who can tread the same line well, as the traditional, wonderfully rude waitresses like Edna retire.

So far there have been mishaps, including the time, according to *The Boston Globe*, that a new, young waitress pulled a customer's glasses off and then 'slapped him on his balding head.' As Queen Victoria might have said, he was not amused (and, in fact, was so enraged he tried to get the offending waitress fired).

The strategy of an enterprise is not a thing apart from its people. Rather the people of any organization enact the enterprise's strategy daily. Whether they do so in ways that create advantage or disavantage is in turn a consequence not of intent, but of investment – of time and money, heart and attention – in who the people are and the decisions they learn to take on the organization's behalf.

Workplace Sizzle

*The executive art is nine-tenths
inducing those who have authority
to use it in taking pertinent action.*

– Chester Barnard
The Functions of the Executive, 1938

Signs when the ability is strong ...
... but the willingness is weak

- Though never stated publicly, the dominant operating philosophy among the most successful managers is that employees are like rubber bands: stretch them until they break, throw them away, and then take another. The rationale is that the company provides enough motivators and sizzle that the future supply of talented staff is virtually inexhaustible.

- Company publications and building corridors are littered with slogans intended to inspire employees, and provide them with a sense of 'glow and tingle' about the company and its products. Meanwhile, most employees – except, of course, the 'newbies' – either ignore the slogans altogether or regard them as a form of 'talkin' trash' ... corporate style.

- Membership is burgeoning in the company's unofficial and underground Aero-Porcine Society (motto: 'we'll do more than the minimum when pigs fly').

- Corporate wisdom says that those employees who have left the company represent no real loss as, in retrospect, they either weren't very good in the first instance or were too difficult to keep over the long haul. Nonetheless, you still have the uneasy feeling that in some cases the assessments are mostly post-exit rationalizations, and that in fact the company has been losing some of its best talent.

- In their exit interviews, most people give similar reasons ... which, by miraculous coincidence, also happen to be the reasons seen as the 'acceptable' rationales for leaving.

- Any internal 'market research' that has been conducted always shows the same things, that the employees are basically happy, but (if anything) would like a bit more money. These findings are no surprise to many of the people surveyed, who are aware that:

  - the questions and response categories were phrased such that only certain issues and answers could emerge,

  - questions touching on issues that could shake up the status quo were excluded, even those (or especially those) that were highly important to employees, or/and

  - they were not able to respond to the questionnaire anonymously.

- Management is very pleased about the increased 'empowerment' of employees. Many of the employees in question also use an e-word for their new status, but the word they use is 'exploitation.'

- A competitor's 'invisible edge' is chalked up to 'attitude,' though no one seems quite sure how to instill this same attitude in the home team.

A bility alone never turned a workforce into a competitive asset. But lack of willingness has turned many workforces
into formidable handicaps, even those with highly capable people serving in intelligently structured roles.

That's precisely the view taken by George Eliot (pen name for
Mary Ann Evans) in her 1866 novel, *Felix Holt*:

> *Fancy what a game of chess would be if all the chessmen had*
> *passions and intellects, more or less small and cunning; if*
> *you were not only uncertain about your adversary's men, but*
> *a little uncertain about your own; if your Knight could shuf-*
> *fle himself on to a new square on the sly; if your Bishop, in*
> *disgust at your Castling, could wheedle your Pawns out of*
> *their places; and if your Pawns, hating you because they are*
> *Pawns, could make away from their appointed posts that you*
> *might get checkmate on a sudden. You might be the longest-*
> *headed of deductive reasoners, and yet you might be beaten by*
> *your own Pawns. You might be especially likely to be beaten,*
> *if you depended on your mathematical imagination, and re-*
> *garded your passionate pieces with contempt.*

A hundred and thirty years later, the point was made again,
though in a radically different setting: a meeting of the
top 437 managers of GE Fanuc Automation North America,
a joint venture between Fanuc Ltd of Japan and the General Electric Company. The speaker in this case was Dr
Michael Hammer, co-author of the best-seller *Reengineering
the Corporation*. As recounted in *The Wall Street Journal*,
Hammer used the GE-Fanuc gathering to admit to a 'flaw'
in reengineering: he and other leaders of the $4.7 billion
reengineering industry 'forgot about people.'

Or as Dr Hammer went on to say:

'There is a great deal of unmapped territory within us which would have to be taken into account in an explanation of our gusts and storms.'
– George Eliot (1819–1880)

> *I wasn't smart enough about that [the 'that' being 'other peo-*
> *ple']. I was reflecting my engineering background and was*

insufficiently appreciative of the human dimension. I've
learned that's critical.

Though separated by time, training, and turn of phrase, both the novelist and the engineer make the same point: if the muscle is strong but the motivation is weak, you still won't achieve your goals. Obvious, right? Well, perhaps. But though I've met few executives who claim you can 'forget about the people,' I've met plenty of other folks who feel that their companies treat them like grocery carts – and who have decreased their work efforts accordingly.

A quick run through the implicit logic shows why this gap in perception prevails. All of us understand that to obtain our customers' commitment, in the form of their money, we need to give them a good deal relative to their alternatives – otherwise, they abandon us in favor of some other option. And most of us understand that for our organizations to receive our personal commitment, each of us, as separate and unique individuals, requires a deal that meets our own needs and wants. It's at the next step in this line of reasoning that things seem to fall apart. That's where observation suggests a common though underground assumption – that motivating other people (as opposed to ourselves, of course) is primarily a matter of providing the right corporate sizzle: a financial package, some fancy words, a set of marching orders, and penalties for failure to comply.

I take the opposite view; more precisely, I hold that motivating other people requires taking the 'good deal at profit over time' framework discussed in the first part of this book, turning it inside out, and applying it to the internal market of employees and employers. Now the employees are the customers. Like all customers, they make payments, but in the internal market they pay in effort rather than in cash. Similarly, the company is still the vendor but in this market the product offerings are composed of 'motivators' – incentives and disincentives. And, finally, within the internal market, the bridge between buyers and sellers shifts from a 'good deal' to a 'fair deal,' because employees tend to use both relative scales and absolute scales in their calculations of how much effort to expend in exchange for the motivators they receive.

If you're pretty sure that such thinking doesn't apply to you because employees in your organization do as they are told, you might check whether you understand the consequences of offering a deal that is widely seen as deficient, as will be discussed in the first part of this chapter. And if you think your company already provides enough of the right kinds of motivators, you might want to reexamine whether you really know what most people in the organization see as an equitable deal, as explored in the second part.

And then you might remember that companies that misunderstand either what they can lose with poor deals on the one hand, or how to construct mutually satisfactory deals on the other, face two unattractive risks. One is becoming victims on George Eliot's chess board. The other is finding themselves charging forward at full throttle … only to realize later how few troops are following in their wake.

Part one
The hidden power of employees …
… and the risk of being
'beaten by your own pawns'

The competitive-game maps introduced in Chapter 3 are a way to visualize a company's position in external markets. I like them because they make it easier to understand causes and consequences of past moves, and to anticipate future moves and reactions. Given this, you won't be surprised that I've also thought about how to draw the fair-deal standard for employee-employer transactions, this time in the form of 'internal-market maps.' But here my purpose is not to plot a company's position relative to its competitors, but rather to visualize the range of possible positions a company can take relative to its employees, and the consequences of each.

In overall structure, internal-market maps are quite similar to their competitive-game map cousins (see Fig. 5.1). Both start with the 'WIF-MEs': the 'what's-in-it-for-mes.' And in both, the WIF-

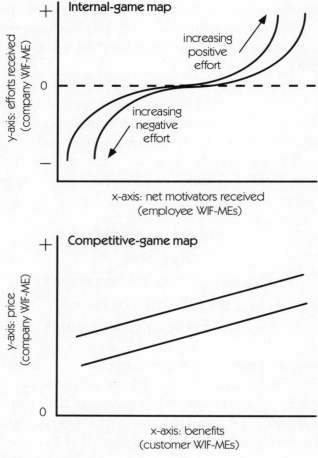

Fig. 5.1 Illustrative curves.

MEs for the company are represented on the y-axis, while
the WIF-MEs for the buyers – in this case, the employees
– are represented on the x-axis. But, as shown in Fig.5.1,
when you plot the most likely combinations of 'product'
offered (the x-axis coordinate) and 'price' paid (the y-
axis coordinate), the resulting curves differ substantially.

For the external market, this curve takes the form of a
rough band, within which all the alternatives are good
deals for their respective customer populations, as described in Chapter 3. From the company's point of view,
which position within the band is 'best' depends on where
the money is and where it's likely to be in the future, and
therefore turns on such factors as relative revenues, relative assets, relative margins, likely growth rates, and the
reserves of imagination and intelligence that can be dedicated to protecting and enhancing the product's position in the
market.

'It depends on if you're pouring or drinking.' – how Bill Cosby's grandmother responded when he asked her the philosophical conundrum, 'Is the glass half full or half empty?'

For the internal markets, though, the band curls both upward
and downward and represents the range of likely positions of all
the participants in a company's workforce. I've drawn this band
as two funnels, to show the multiplier effect that occurs when
employees think they are getting really good deals – or really rot-
ten ones. Now better and worse are clearly defined by location.
The better positions are in the upright funnel in the northeast
quadrant of the map; the further north, the more working hard
and working smart becomes contagious, and the greater the potential advantage a company can achieve relative to its
competitors. In a similar way, every position in the up-
side-down funnel in the southwest quadrant is bad, and
the further south, the greater the damage.

'Bloom, damn you, bloom!' – note written by W.C. Fields to recalitrant rose bushes in his garden

Now step back and look at the internal-market map as
a whole. What's displayed here is a visual representation
of the hidden power of employees; the power of each person *to choose* how well to do his or her job; to be able to
decide, a hundred or so times a day, whether to take a

step forward or to withhold effort, even when the ability to do more is present. It's a substantial power, one that can humble the mighty and enhance the humble.

Three factors contribute to this hidden power. One is each person's ability to vary how much effort to contribute above and beyond whatever is seen as the minimum level tolerated. The second is the flipside of the first; each person's ability to harm the enterprise, and to do so in ways that either aren't seen or can't be prevented. And the third is the difficulty of detecting when employee effort is going south in time to take corrective actions.

1. The 'less than desired' factor: why the hidden power of employees is an accountant's nightmare

In markets composed of transactions between a company and its external customers, buyers exercise power during negotiations. Then, for any combination of price (as shown on the y-axis) and bundle of benefits (as listed on the x), they make yes/no decisions; they either buy or they don't buy. And when they buy, the payments they make are fixed, visible, and measurable. This is a nice world for accountants. Once negotiations are over, they know how much cash they can expect and when it's supposed to arrive; later, at the time of payment, they can count it, bank it, and incorporate it into their financial statements.

In markets composed of transactions between employees and employers, though, employees can and do decide to vary the payments they make well after the negotiations are over. In consequence, even when most of the people in a workforce know what to do and how to do it, they can still choose to do less, independent of what's in their paychecks. More complicated still, in these internal markets, such payment decisions are made continuously, making both the assessments and the payments variable rather than fixed.

This is an accountant's nightmare – a blurry and constantly shifting stream of payments, most of which can't be predicted with any precision because they are made on an implicit and shifting sliding scale; kind of an installment plan gone Wonderland. Unlike the world of external transactions, where payments are received, recorded, and then reserved for future use, most of these payments behave in exactly the opposite way. Individually, they are difficult to see and virtually impossible to measure in real time – even by the most eagle-eyed accountant or supervisor. And they are perishable: companies can bank good will, but they can't bank effort.

The temptation, when confronted by an accountant's nightmare such as this one, is to ignore what can't be counted, and therefore to assume the effort paid will be the same as the effort desired. And that in turn will almost guarantee that the real effort paid out will be grossly misestimated.

'I admit that twice two makes four is an excellent thing, but if we are to give everything its due, twice two makes five is sometimes a very charming thing too.'
– Feodor Dostoevski (1821–1881)

2. The 'worse than imagined' factor: why the hidden power of employees is a chessmaster's nightmare

Not only are the actual transactions in the external market easier to see and track than those in the internal market, the dynamics of customer power are also more transparent: Customers have more power when they have more vendors and more good alternatives from which to make their selections. At these times, they are choosier simply because they can be. Conversely, when markets are effectively closed to all but a few competitors, customers have less power and have to make do with the best of what's available to them, no matter how bad. In all cases, the buyers have some hidden ability to do harm – they can badmouth their vendors and store up their grievances until the day a new competitor strolls into town – but by and large they are captive to the explicit power dynamics of the situation.

In the internal market of employee–employer transactions, the dynamics are murkier. Clearly, when labor markets are tight, prospective and current employees can negotiate better packages of pay and working conditions; conversely, when there are more people than jobs to be had, the balance of power shifts to the employers. But this is where the second aspect of the hidden power of employees comes into play. Labor markets are sticky; perceptions of risk and disruption mean that many employees stay in jobs they don't like and work for companies they don't respect. Others leave of their own volition, but part with bad feelings. Both types of disgruntled employees have multiple ways of creating incremental costs and other disadvantages for their current or former employers – should they wish to use them. Here are just a few

Divorce, corporate style

When employees leave a company, whether voluntarily or under duress, there are some obvious savings and obvious costs. The savings occur when positions are truly eliminated, or when new people are hired but at lower wages and/or with less generous benefits than their predecessors received. The costs include the expenses of recruiting and training people when replacements are required. Often left out of the calculations, however, are the losses of what resides only in cranium-space.

Consider who's likely to leave an organization. First are the people who believe they have the most labor mobility. These are the folks who quit when they think they can find a better deal on the outside than what they currently have. They're also the ones who quickly take the buy-out packages that are aimed at clearing the deadwood out of an organization but, like misguided neutron bombs, leave the deadwood in place while eradicating the movers and shakers. And they're the people who have enormous reserves of information, ideas, intuitions, and instincts stuffed in their heads. Even with the best of will and the most efficient technology, no company can hope to retain more than a small fraction of these invisible assets; the rest evaporates when the employee walks out the door.

Second are the people who are asked to leave, casualties in companies' efforts to rightsize, reengineer, restructure or otherwise downsize. But often these are also the people who were part of the informal systems of how things really got done; without them, redesigns that looked good on paper sometimes fall apart after the new schemes go live. In some companies, the solution used has not been without its comical aspects: hire back the people laid off, sometimes with better financial packages than before. Imagine what that does for morale.

Parting shots

Just because a person has been severed from a company doesn't prevent the firing of parting shots aimed at evening the score. In some cases, the method of choice is a law suit, a tactic more common in the US than elsewhere. More frequently, however, it's to share insights and information with competitors – not only what's in the person's head – but also what can be hidden in a jacket pocket, beamed out electronically, or even put on a Web site.

With technology, in fact, it's easier than ever for those unhappy about how they have been treated to take their revenge. At one American high-tech company, a departing senior scientist wiped his hard disk clean of data that had taken years to assemble – and for which the company had no complete backup – and then, for good measure, disabled the hardware to ensure that data restoration techniques couldn't put back together what he had just torn asunder.

Or consider the classic saga of the executive in the finance department of oil giant, Texaco Inc. Informed in 1996 that he was being let go by the company, this ex-manager decided to give a small audio cassette filled with incriminating conversations to a group of plaintiffs suing his now-former employer for race discrimination. Cash cost to Texaco: a one-time $176.1 million settlement, the largest in US legal history for a case of this kind. Additional cost to Texaco: subordination to a seven-person 'equality and tolerance' task force with broad powers to control the company's personnel policies, to which the company can appoint only three of the seven members. (The chairman is jointly appointed by the two parties, and the plaintiffs appoint the other three.) Revenge in this case may not have been sweet, as the tapes also incriminated the whistle blower, but it sure was effective.

'Nothing on earth consumes a man more quickly than the passion of resentment.'
– Friedrich Nietzsche (1844–1900)

On-the-job shoe jamming

Not leaving your job, but still unhappy and want to make a point of it? No problem. Just remember the French workers of a century or so ago who, when particularly displeased, used to jam their wooden shoes (called sabots) into their employers' machinery, thereby giving rise to the word 'sabotage' for an age-old phenomenon that crosses national boundaries with ease.

At one extreme are those on-the-job saboteurs whose efforts to cause embarrassment are quite visible, even if they themselves remain invisible. Examples include, years ago, people who reportedly stuffed miniature sex manuals as prizes in boxes of Crackerjacks snack food, and American auto-workers who put the odd bolt into dead spaces of cars to create infuriating rattles. These are the obvious acts of sabotage, inflicted by people who have little or no respect for the companies for which they work and whose efforts to harm are quite evident – even if they themselves remain anonymous.

More common, and far more insidious, though, are the people who conduct acts of sabotage that, though harmful, are almost impossible to detect. This was the situation in the case of a junior bank officer who, when customers called with complaints, routinely listened attentively, carefully wrote down all the concerns, assured the customers that she would take care of the problem – and then, as soon as she hung up the phone or the customer was out of sight, would wad the paper up into a ball, toss it into her waste basket, and promptly forget about both the complaint and the complainer. She has since been promoted several times. (The customers, on the other hand, would become increasingly enraged at the bank – but, not of course, at the 'nice young lady' who had 'tried so hard' to help them.) Other people sabotage operations simply by making it 'uncool' to work hard, or by conducting whispering campaigns amongst fellow employees or with customers. Even virtual shoes can still jam up the works.

Slow-down at the OK Corral

Sabotage is a covert expression of job dissatisfaction. But sometimes the selected means of expressing the view is to make the retaliation explicit. This was the approach taken by a group of Girl Scouts at about the same time that Dr Hammer was regaling the top 437 managers of GE Fanuc Automation North America with his newly found appreciation of 'the human dimension.' In particular, these Girl Scouts, who hailed from Laurel, New Jersey, were less than pleased about the distribution of proceeds from the cookies they were selling door to door as part of the Scouts' fundraising activities.

It seems that for each $3.00 box the girls sold, 81¢ was going to the bakery and $1.69 to the Girl Scout governing council, which left only 50¢ for local activities. The girls thought this was unfair, and made an alternate proposal: if headquarters would reduce their take to $1.59 and add the residual 10¢ per box to the local pot, the troops would guarantee increased sales. And then – just to make sure that everyone was clear on their concept – these sweet little girls staged a work slow-down. The net result: everybody lost, but the Scouts themselves got an early lesson in

'A little rebellion now and then is a good thing. It is medicine for the sound health of government.'

– Thomas Jefferson (1734–1826), drafter of the Declaration of Independence and third president of the United States how to fight back when you think the rules of the internal game have been unfairly stacked against you.

Work slow-downs are in fact the most common, and often least visible, of all revenges: care a little less, do a little less, frequently while smiling nicely. When undertaken by one or just a handful of people, such revenges are a nuisance. Undertaken by most people in the workforce for most of their hundred decisions a day, and they create invisible liabilities of immense magnitude.

Shoot-out at the Lusty Lady

And finally, there's another option in on-going battle to keep the power lines in balance: unionization. And it's not just for old-line manufacturing concerns anymore, as demonstrated by the exotic dancers at the Lusty Lady Club in San Francisco who, when management refused to enforce a no-filming rule, decided to form a bargaining unit. The precipitating event: illicit video tapes of the dancers were ending up on the Internet, and the dancers, most of whom hadn't provided their parents and friends with complete or accurate details about their working lives, were worried about the possibility of surprise revelations. (As one dancer confided to *The Boston Globe*, 'My parents are Catholics and live on the east coast … they would be crushed.') They also wanted days off for illness, a 'modest' health plan, minimum working hours, and 'elimination of favoritism' in promotions.

The dancers prevailed and, by a vote of 57 to 15, became members of the Service Employees International Union (SEIU), Local 790, making The Lusty Lady Club the first union strip club in the United States. The dancers also launched an Internet home page providing accurate and practical advice for other exotic dancers and sex workers wishing to unionize, along with warnings about pitfalls in the process. (Sample: 'Expect management to lie, manipulate history and "the facts." If you work for unsavory sleazeballs, their behavior won't shock you. But if you're used to cordial honesty from your employer, it may be hard to get used to routine deceit.')

Now, here's what's interesting to me about the certification of SEIU Local 790. In 1996, at the time of the dancers' unionization drive, US companies saw their power as most absolute. Downsizing and reengineering had become national manias. The country was experiencing phenomenal economic strength, due in part to its relative labor flexibility. And organized labor was declared to be dead, or at least irrelevant and on its way to dying.

But while many managers were discounting the power of organized labor, two counter forces were gaining momentum. One was that many people – even those who had not been downsized, rightsized, reengineered or otherwise restructured out of their jobs or pushed into less attractive ones – were feeling that the increased prosperity was going disproportionately to shareholders and top executives. And the other was that the National Labor Relations Board, the governmental body that regulates union certification in the United States, was more pro-labor that it had been in several decades.

When you put the pieces together, an interesting picture emerges. Temporary and contract workers had begun to talk about finding ways to overcome existing regulatory obstacles to unionization. Professors in universities were signing union cards; so were physicians in the nation's internship and residency training programs. White collars workers in many industries were thinking about whether they needed union protection, many for the first time. The Teamsters struck UPS over 'corporate greed' and most of the American public supported the union, which won concessions from the company. All of this gives rise to an interesting question: why would managers of US companies invite further unionization by treating their employees as though they were grocery carts or rubber bands, rather than human beings? Why would managers in any country do so?

'You cannot do a kindness too soon, for you never know when it will be too late.' – Ralph Waldo Emerson (1803– 1882), American author and philosopher

George Eliot was right. Power is never absolute; those with less power – even the lowliest of Pawns – can still 'make away from their appointed posts that you might get checkmate on a

sudden.' People who forget her words in favor of the conven-
ient belief that 'employees who don't like things around here
can just leave,' are often in for a rude surprise, one that is all the
more unpleasant for being an outcome of their own making.

3. The 'hits you before you see it' factor: the leader's nightmare and the search for the coal miners' canary

The third aspect of the hidden power of employees is how difficult it is to assess when a company isn't getting what it needs –
and why – until it's too late. One way to picture this situation is
to take another look at the Internal-Market Map, now focusing
on the inflexion or crossover point, as illustrated in Fig. 5.2.

The crossover point in the middle of the map provides a conceptual divider between positive efforts made on an employer's
behalf, and those that are negative in nature. The question is
whether you can see when people are sliding toward or beyond
the crossover point. After all, the best saboteurs leave no footprints. And how do you measure the hidden costs incurred by

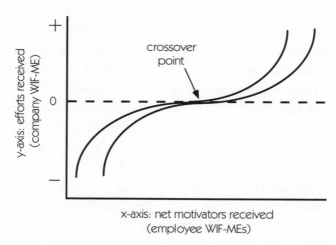

Fig. 5.2 Crossover point on the internal-market map.

people who care a little less and do a little less, but do so in subtle, subvert ways? A common answer to my questions goes like this: 'I know that people can modify the amount and quality of effort they give. But this isn't a problem for us, because we do yearly surveys of our employees, plus we conduct selected exit interviews when people leave, so we have advance notice of any incipient problems in time to fix them.' In effect, they believe that their research provides them with virtual canaries, the organizational equivalent of the real canaries used by coal miners a century ago to determine whether it was safe to work (if the canary died, the miners knew it was time to vamoose, and fast).

The problem is that while live canaries provide an accurate read of rising carbon monoxide levels, employees surveys and exit interviews often obscure the signs of rising dissatisfaction within the workforce – and of declines in effort paid out in response. The reason is fairly straightforward; as used in many organizations, both are exercises in irrelevance and prevarication.

The irrelevance comes from survey designs that wouldn't – or shouldn't, at least – pass muster in any introductory research course. Take a look at the last few surveys done in your organization. How many of the questions are of the 'do you love your mother' variety – that is, questions for which it would be difficult to give anything other than the expected answer – or other boilerplate questions that invite boilerplate responses? (Example: 'Do you support the mission of this company?' – 'Yes.') Conversely, how many of the questions reflect the issues that employees are talking about – in their e-mails, over the watercooler, and at other assorted odd moments? And if you said that the questions in the surveys used in your organization have a high relevance quotient, how would you know?

Which brings us to the question of prevarication. It's a simple rule that the more risk there is in an honest answer, the higher the odds that a dishonest one will be given. Now, consider the circumstances of both those people who a company currently employs, and those who are leaving. Why should people in either of these groups give accurate answers to tough questions – unless they are certain that negative answers can't be traced back to them?

In the case of the currently employed, the jeopardy is direct retribution; and no matter how convinced you are that your company has an open environment, anyone who sees their paycheck at risk will view the situation from a slightly different – and more vulnerable – perspective. In the case of those who are leaving, the smart ones know the world is a small place – especially when it comes to references and reputations. Better to tell the interviewers what they want to hear than bother with the truth. The usual way to do this is to give whatever the accepted reason is for that group (money, travel, time for family – depending on the rationale most salient to the people asking the questions).

> 'A straw vote shows only which way the hot air blows.
> – O. Henry (1862–1910), American author

And then there are the people who go further, and thereby take their place in the Exit-Interview Whoppers Hall of Fame. A few of my favorites: A man, who was leaving a prestigious company, tells the top boss that his father is dying and he has to take over his business. (Real story: his dad was fine, but the departing employee had been interviewing for a while, and had just found his dream job.) A woman, leaving another company, tearfully tells her boss that she has to leave as her husband has just accepted a position in another city. (Real story: her husband scrambled to find a job in the new city after his wife found hers – but before she told her employer.) In each case, the boss bought the line, allowing both sides to save face, but ensuring that the real issues remained unexposed.

There is another way, however. And that's to start by trying to understand the real deal – as seen by the employees.

Part two
The art of the deal:
building blocks that add and subtract

For about four decades, starting after World War II, pollster Daniel Yankelovich embarked on a research journey to figure out what working people in the US want, and whether they will give more to get more. With colleagues, he conducted similar studies in Japan, Germany, Israel, Sweden, and the United Kingdom. Across time and culture, two findings stand out. One is that a significant number of people would invest more in their jobs, if the companies they work for would make it worth their while to do so. The other is that while money is important, it is only one component of the deal between employers and employees.

But, if a fair deal in the internal market takes more than money, what other WIF-MEs are required? The research done by Yankelovich and his colleagues provides a great start. I've combined those data with my own observations to compile this list of a few key motivators:

- *the pay-mes:*   the financial package
- *the give-mes:*   work conditions that make the job more agreeable
- *the let-mes:*   amount of discretion permitted in the conduct of the job
- *the assist-mes:*   investment in ensuring the job is doable
- *the respect-mes:*   treatment on the job on a day-to-day basis
- *the brand-mes:*   image imparted by being part of this company
- *the convince-mes:* confidence in management to lead the company

Some of these motivators – particularly, the *pay-me*s and *give-me*s – are highly amenable to numerical scales; most are not.

And, just as in external markets, different people attribute different levels of importance to each – with variations occurring within companies, between companies within countries, and between countries. But all of them make a difference – either by adding to an employee's 'willingness account,' or subtracting from it. And all of them provide the basis for trade-offs in which people accept decrements in one benefit order to score larger gains in others that are more valuable and salient to them.

A brief overview of these WIF-MEs follows, conducted in the form of questions and commentaries. Each question is posed as a broad statement with a rating scale based on how much you agree or disagree with the statement. If you're willing, pencil in your answers as you read along – and then think about how others in your organization might answer the same questions.

The PAY-MEs:

Question 1   I get fair financial compensation for the effort I am asked to expend.

Rating scale: (disagree strongly) 0_____10 (agree strongly)

The temptation, when doing maps of either external markets or those within a firm, is to define the x-axis by a numerical scale. Starting with competitive-game maps for external markets, the theory is that numbers put everything on an apples-to-apple basis. This isn't so bad if you're making applesauce, but otherwise leads to boring meals. It also guarantees that you will miss – or, at minimum, underestimate – benefits that customers value, especially the intangibles. For this reason, as discussed in Chapter 3, I like to use words to describe the x-axis, and divide it into tickets-to-play (the TTPs), and various levels of differentiators.

With internal-market maps, though, the desire to use numbers for the x-axis is even stronger. Take current compensation, add the financial value of other company-paid benefits such as retirement and sick leave, and *voilà!* – the perfect set of numbers to use as a benchmark for whether the deal is adequate or not.

There are two problems with this approach. One is that not all people optimize their lives to achieve the highest possible compensation (investment bankers excepted, of course). The Yankelovich data show this, and so does simple observation. The other is that though compensation numbers are absolute, appraisals of fairness are relative.

'Not everything that can be counted counts, and not everything that counts can be counted.' – Albert Einstein (1879–1955)

Consider the following scenario. A company commissions a compensation study to ensure that wages and benefit packages for the rank and file fits within industry norms. The target is somewhere around the fiftieth percentile or perhaps a little more, and the compensation packages for employees who are earning appreciably less than this target are adjusted accordingly. Then the Compensation Committee of the Board commissions a similar study for the top executives of the company. But now the target is set at the seventy-fifth percentile or above – after all, what board members would want to admit that the CEO of *their* company was 'only average'? Multiply this scenario across many companies over a number of years, and you'll see widening pay gaps between the rank and file and top managers – gaps of on the order of a 100–200-times magnitude in many US companies.

Such gaps can and do have a corrosive effect, especially in times of corporate belt-tightenings, restructurings, and downsizings. That's when conversations in the press and on corporate premises turn to the topic of 'corporate greed.' Part of the issue is absolute numbers ('I want more'), but part of it is relative ('it's not fair') – and it's this perception of relative lack of fairness that can send employees leftward on the x-axis (less WIF-MEs for me), and therefore downward on the y-axis (less effort for you).

The GIVE-MEs

Question 2 The overall conditions here are quite reasonable.
Rating scale: (disagree strongly) 0_____10 (agree strongly)

The deal between employers and employees includes a number of work conditions that translate directly into financial costs to the company, and are either positive or negative motivators to employees. To list just a few of the obvious ones: cleanliness of workplace, safety, availability of on-premises cafeterias, food quality, workplace location, availability of parking. Others include office configurations, travel rules, training programs, and flexibility in work hours and schedules.

Most of these attributes are monotonic; that is, just about everyone prefers a safer workplace, better food, and nicer work spaces. But not all of them are. A prime example of one that isn't is telecommuting. Many companies like telecommuters because they lead to lower real-estate costs. Some employees also love the set up, as they vastly prefer working from home, being accountable for output rather than face time, and operating with high levels of flexibility. Many of these people are unmarried, young, and technologically hip. Other telecommuters, though, are miserable. Their family situations make working at home difficult at best, plus they miss the social interactions that are part of a communal work space. For them, the cost cutting that reduces corporate expenses for space also takes a major bite out of the WIF-MEs they get from working for the company.

For the remainder of the attributes, the ones for which the preference of almost all employees go in a similar direction, companies face interesting choices. Consider travel policy. Companies can save a heap of money by limiting the choice of airlines to only those with which it has cut special deals. Such arrangements often require taking flights leaving at inconvenient times and changing planes rather than flying non-stop, all of which result in extra hassle and frustration – not to mention the extra travel time – which in turn ultimately come out of time that the employee could have devoted to other, non-work activities. From the company's point of view, the savings can be compelling; from the employee's, they can range anywhere from mildly irritating to highly abusive.

Or let's go back to office space. Some companies have eliminated offices altogether in favor of desk-sharing, which they've then dressed up with the unusually clunky euphemism of 'hoteling.' Others engage in the fabulous 'shrinking-cubicle' game; at one company, the office betting pool was on when a pregnant colleague would no longer be able to fit into her workspace. The bet depended on predicting two conflicting forces; her naturally increasing girth, and the company's constant effort to 're-size' (read: reduce) all cubicles in the building.

'He [Robert Benchley] and I had an office so tiny that an inch smaller and it would have been adultery.' – Dorothy Parker (1893–1967), American author

What's sauce for the goose, though, isn't always sauce for the gander. At one major accounting firm, partners were called 'long-term hotelers' and were therefore said to have 'long-term reservations' – or what the rest of us would call permanent offices. Explained the firm's spokesman to *The Boston Globe*, 'To make the idea work, we called everyone a hoteler so no one was perceived as being excused from the system. It was a kind of mind over matter thing.' Right.

At another company, a new-age guru convinced the CEO to redesign the executive floor into an open office plan, with the perimeter of the floor dedicated to secretarial bays, and the interior divided into gigantic cubicles, with each executive occupying a suite composed of large office plus a large conference room – all entered via big doorways that, naturally, had no doors. But the executives didn't much like living in the wide open interior spaces of the building, and as soon as the renovations were complete, began having meetings at a satellite facility, just outside the city, where a set of conventional offices and meeting rooms were available. Travel to the second facility stopped when the executive floor was restored to its previous configuration, demonstrating once again that even when you can't see them in a paycheck, the *give-me*s can be highly important – no matter where you sit in an organization.

The LET-MEs, ASSIST-MEs, and RESPECT-MEs

Question 3   I get the chance to think for myself rather than just carry out instructions.

Rating scale: (disagree strongly) 0_____10 (agree strongly)

Question 4   It may take hard work, but I'm confident my job can be done well.

Rating scale: (disagree strongly) 0_____10 (agree strongly)

Question 5   The people I work with and for treat me with respect.

Rating scale: (disagree strongly) 0_____10 (agree strongly)

At a meeting in Montréal, I was seated next to a well-known labor attorney who represented management for some of Quebec's most prestigious companies. Over the course of the conversation, I asked him what he saw as the root of the labor disputes he saw. 'It is simple,' he replied. 'In almost every case, it starts with treating the workers as widgets rather than as people.' A leading US labor attorney who similarly sits on management's side of the table seconded the observation.

How do companies avoid the employees-as-widgets trap? I think at least three components are involved. One is allowing employees to use their brains as they do their jobs, the *'let-mes.'* That makes the work more interesting, and gives the people more explicit control over what they do. But now the costs are personal, because they require sharing power and sharing credit, rather than spending the company's cash. This leads to an interesting dilemma. Most managers love the idea of empowerment, especially when they hear the tales that have passed into business-theory folklore, such as how employees at Microsoft moved heaven and earth to bring the company from behind in the Internet wars. Fewer, however, are keen to actually share *their* power to get such results, which is the lesson I take from the Greek myth about Prometheus. (The thumb-nail version: Prometheus gave humankind fire by stealing *one* coal from Zeus' hearth. Zeus responded by chaining Prometheus to a mountain for eternity and arranging for a hungry vulture to dine daily on Prometheus' liver.) In current times, more than a few bosses have reacted similarly when asked to share power as part of their companies' empowerment efforts.

Second are the *'assist-mes'*, ensuring that the jobs are doable with reasonable effort; otherwise employees find themselves caught between unrealistic rhetoric on the one hand, and unachievable goals on the other. In part this means making sure that the right people are in the right jobs; in part it means investing in on-the-job coaching plus other kinds of training; and in part it means making a real commitment to removing the organizational obstacles that block productive work. How big are such costs? Take another look at the case studies in Chapter 4 on the Boston Four Seasons and the BI; both organizations have made huge investments in time and attention to help people do their job well. They also reap huge paybacks for their efforts.

And finally, there's what should be the simple issue of treating people with courtesy – or what I call the *'respect-mes'* – a costly matter for those who derive part of their personal identity from their relative status in the organization's hierarchy (whether this hierarchy is accurately portrayed on the company's org charts or not). For these people, being polite to those with less power is seen as quite unnecessary; more to the point, for some, the ability to be impolite and still get one's wishes is a key psychic perk of the job. In most cases of this type, the usual response is to acquiesce in public – and seethe in private.

'A lot of top managers enjoy cruelty. But the financial benefit they get for layoffs is morally and socially unforgivable, and we'll pay a very nasty price.'
– Peter Drucker, in an interview with *Wired* magazine

But not always. Consider the encounter between a new resident (post-graduate position for physicians) at a prestigious academic medical center and a senior doctor, who turned out to be the Chief Resident, a man used to total, unquestioned obedience from everyone junior to him in rank. In this case, the Chief Resident walked up to the new resident, interrupted her as she was working with a patient and a group of medical students, and barked out a wholly inappropriate order, without even introducing himself. When the new resident stood her ground, the astonished Chief Resident drew himself up to his full six foot plus height and thundered, 'do you know who I am?' At which point the new resident paused, eyed her questioner, and responded 'As nearly as I can tell, you're just a big jerk' (although she in fact used a anatomical descriptor). I am told that the residents, medical students and nurses watching the spectacle raised a silent cheer. More cheers came later when at the end of her training, this woman earned the honor of being the Chief Resident.

Investments in the *let-mes*, *assist-mes*, and *respect-mes* are seldom identified on a company's financial statements. Yet the consequences always end up in the bottom line. In fact, according to the Yankelovich surveys, job attributes related to being treated like people rather than widgets are the ones that are most important to people in the US workforce – even as compared to opportunities to maximize income. So here are a few questions to consider: To what extent does your organization provide the *let-mes*, *assist-mes*, and *respect-mes*? Do the levels provided add the people's willingness to pay attention and put extra effort into their jobs? Or do they detract from the overall deal, and leave many in the workforce less interested in doing any more than the bare minimum?

The BRAND-MEs and CONVINCE-MEs:

Question 6   I get a great feeling of pride when I tell people where I work.

Rating scale: (disagree strongly) 0_____10 (agree strongly)

Question 7   I have high confidence in the team leading this company.

Rating scale: (disagree strongly) 0_____10 (agree strongly)

Pride and confidence are wonderful motivators. The *brand-me*s and the *convince-me*s can provide both of these, but do so in almost completely mirror image ways.

The *brand-me*s confer pride and confidence by virtue of past performance. They also convey a kind of halo effect. If a company's name is strong in its external markets, it probably will also enhance the reputations of those who work there. There's more referred status (and snob appeal) in working at Sumitomo Bank than at the Somerville Savings and Loan Company; ditto for Marks and Spencer versus Emma's Roadside Emporium or Mercedes versus Yugo. In fact, for some people, the *brand-me*s compensate for any number of sins: bad treatment, long hours, poor work conditions. But, over the long haul, the *brand-me*s are also transient – who would have thought that being a part of Microsoft or SAP would be more prestigious than working at WordPerfect or even IBM, that Cadillac would seem declassé relative to a name plate – Lexus – in the Toyota family of cars, or that a company called Virgin could be uttered in the same breath as British Airways?

The *convince-me*s, on the other hand, operate as future values. They confer pride and confidence by virtue of each individual's assessment of whether management has a clue as to what the future holds and how to navigate given the obvious uncertainties. The *convince-me*s, in fact, were a large part of the reason I wrote *Fad Surfing in the Boardroom*. My contention was, and remains, that many executives have responded to anxieties about the future by taking the equivalent of 'managerial Prozac': a sequence of managerial fads thrown together with little attention to what each technique can produce or what story is being conveyed, thereby confusing being busy with being productive. The result: reduction in anxiety for the sponsors – and radical devaluation of the *convince-me*s for the rest of the organization.

Some theorists call this 'glow and tingle' and claim that it motivates employees. I call it rubbish. In the middle ages, people could gather at the great cathedrals and follow the stories told in the stained glass windows or in the tapestries. If you try to do the same today with all the programs any single company has implemented over the past few years, you're more likely to end up with something that looks like a Jackson Pollock canvas – splatters of paint everywhere but nothing resembling a storyline. Given this, why would anyone believe that the effect of such random clutter would be anything other than to convince large groups of people that those at the top of the pyramid are clueless? And why would anyone put in much more than the minimum if they are placing their work fates in the hands of such obviously impaired leaders?

Clearly, different people have different profiles; labor pools break into segments just as external markets do. For some, for example, a great financial package and an interesting job will make up for low scores on the *convince-me*s, and vice versa. But the overall point still holds: providing what the internal market sees as a fair deal can unlock the willingness factor which, when married to ability, can put a firm far ahead of its competitors. Now, take another look at how you answered the seven questions posed in the headers of this chapter and consider how the rest of the people in your organization might answer them. And then ask yourself the bonus question: what makes you think that your firm is meeting the collective WIF-MEs of its unique constituencies?

'Our deeds determine us as much as we determine our deeds.'

– George Eliot

• • •

If you want a really good vantage point for viewing the Boston skyline at night, visit the campus of the Massachusetts Institute of Technology. From there, you look across the Charles River to the elegant nineteenth-century townhouses, the beautiful church spires, the golden dome of the State House, and the sleek profile of I.M. Pei's Hancock Tower. Most of the time, you will also see the huge red neon 'Sheraton' sign that sits – naturally enough – atop the Sheraton hotel. Except for one week a year. That's the time of MIT's 'Rush Week' when, by tradition, members of the MIT chapter of the ATO fraternity dress in black clothes, paint their faces in camouflage make-up, grab plans they have carefully crafted over the preceding weeks, cross the river by bridge, stealthily avoid hotel security to reach prearranged posts, and rewire the sign to read 'ATO.' They then make their escape and place bets on how many days their letters stay lit. (ATO brothers are proud of the fact that they can usually do their 'hack,' as practical jokes at MIT are called, without harm. If they do break something, however, they tape a fraternity check to whatever they damaged. After all, this is the MIT chapter of ATO, and there are standards to be maintained.)

A few years ago, the incoming ATO president – a budding reengineer, perhaps – decided he had a more efficient idea: call the hotel and ask them to change the sign during Rush Week. No problem, he was told, and that was that. Guess what happened the next year, when my friend Larry took over as president of the fraternity? That's right: on the appointed night, ATO brothers put on their grubbiest black duds, painted their faces with camouflage make-up, grabbed the plans they had crafted over the preceding weeks, entered the hotel surreptitiously, and went about executing the newest set of plans to rewire the appearance of the Boston skyline. The thrill was in the degree of challenge, first and foremost.

People like Larry sit on the far extreme of the *let-me*s. Jobs that give them a bit of control over what they are asked to do will never be satisfying; what they really want are challenges, the bigger the better, and the ability to create elegant solutions to complicated problems. When they find jobs like this, they keep finding ways to help push their companies ahead as Larry has at the company he joined upon graduation.

Managers wishing for an army of Larrys, who therefore decide to reengineer their companies' processes or invest in new 'empowerment' programs, might first take a deep breath and then look at the individuals in their workforces. Different people desire different levels of the *let-me*s, just as they do for all the WIF-MEs that companies can provide. For some, the desire is for a bit of control and with it, a limited amount of responsibility. For others, like Larry, anything less than a substantial challenge and a great deal of accountability is boring, a characteristic devoutly to be avoided.

If George Eliot was right, and all chessmen have passions and intellects, then it makes sense to understand what these preferences are and how to meet them. For while the reengineers may have forgotten about 'the human dimension,' the rest of us know that people who think they are getting a fair deal will do more for their employers than those who believe they are being taken for granted, exploited, or otherwise treated less well than they reckon they should be.

Section 3

The Sins of Information

This is the conversation that Lewis Carroll imagined over a century ago:

> 'When I use a word,' Humpty Dumpty said, in rather a scornful tone, 'it means just what I choose it to mean – neither more nor less.'
> 'The question is,' said Alice, 'whether you can make words mean so many different things.'
> 'The question is,' said Humpty Dumpty, 'which is to be master – that's all.'

This point of view may sound odd coming from an egg. Yet it exactly illustrates how many managers handle information from and about the marketplace; as intrusions to be beaten into submission rather than as signposts that can indicate when it's time to check key assumptions or modify the current direction. Then organizations that could have done better don't, much to the chagrin of their stakeholders and delight of their competitors.

With data, as with strategy and people, the path to corporate purgatory is paved with good intentions. Which brings us to the final two of our septet of sins. These are the Deadly Sins of Information, and they read as follows:

- Sin #6: Taking pride in being a learning organization ... even though key decision makers are unable or unwilling to see the facts for the creed.

- Sin #7: Investing in sophisticated forward intelligence systems ... while consistently falling backward in the battles that count.

Such sins can be the most harmful of all, because they protect the prevailing 'truths' inherent in the first five. But perhaps it's worth letting Humpty Dumpty get the next to last word in:

> 'Impenetrability! That's what I say!'
> 'Would you tell me, please,' said Alice, 'what that means?'
> 'Now you talk like a reasonable child,' said Humpty Dumpty, looking very much pleased. 'I meant by "impenetrability" that we've had enough of that subject, and it would be just as well if you'd mention what you mean to do next, as I suppose you don't mean to stop here all the rest of your life.'
> 'That's a great deal to make one word mean,' Alice said in a thougtful tone.
> 'When I make a word do a lot of work like that,' said Humpty Dumpty, 'I always pay it extra.'

All managers can make data mean what they want them to mean; the question is, what will the extra costs be and who will have to pay them?

Learning Organization

If the facts don't fit the theory,
change the facts.

– Albert Einstein

Signs when your organization has committed to learning ... ... but can't see the facts for the creed

- Data massage has been raised to such a fine art that the company could open a health-club subsidiary for data that have become wayward or otherwise unsightly to those who hold the power.

- No data massage is required at your organization because:

  - all the data are exactly as expected, all the time.

  - the only data that don't fit the expected pattern are 'outliers,' which shouldn't be considered anyway.

  - the last person who brought data that made people feel uncomfortable subsequently discovered that he had been transferred to the East Overshoe regional office ... or the nearest career equivalent thereof.

- The implicit management model in your company is to start with the conclusions, and then fit in the facts. This provides a highly efficient way to process information (although, on occasion, it does require a bit of effort to redefine the questions or reinterpret the data to make sure that everything fits with the expected answers).

- When confronted with an unexpected finding that simply will not be explained away, the most common response is 'that's the exception that proves the rule.' No one has ever questioned the meaning of such a patently stupid expression.

- Your company prides itself on its collegial, comfortable environment. Therefore anyone who insists on talking about information that makes others either vaguely uncomfortable or visibly angry has violated the rules about congeniality and is to be ostracized until significant and sustained improvement is noted. (Also see previous notation regarding the East Overshoe office.)

- Though you sometimes feel like you've been blindsided by changes in the marketplace that your competitors have already used to their own advantage, you can't figure out how such a terrible (and terribly unfair) outcome has come to pass.

- If your company had a patron saint, it would be Tinkerbell. That's because management's interpretation of the facts most closely corresponds to what readers of *Peter Pan* were asked to do to keep Tinkerbell alive: clap three times and say 'I believe, I believe.' It worked in Never-Never Land; why not at your company?

Observation is the foundation of all learning. The scientific method depends on it. Medical diagnosis starts with it. And without it, Boyd's formulation of observation–orientation–decision–action would be one O short of a full loop.

But accurate observation is more difficult than one might first imagine. The villains are two perceptual lenses that act as distorting filters: our expectations and our preferences. Singly and in combination they can lull us into thinking that we know what the data say, when in actuality what we're seeing is what we expect and prefer to see, rather than what's right in front of us.

Just how much distortion these twin lenses can cause was brought home to me the day I was walking down a street in Boston, and found myself fascinated by an unfolding tableau. In the center of my field of vision were four of the most gorgeous men I had ever seen, in running shorts, jogging in what looked to be a two-by-two formation. Behind them was a scrawny fellow, looking more like Charlie Chaplin than Arnold Schwarzenegger, who was alternately sprinting after the four, then slowing down to catch his breath. When he finally caught up with one of the runners, he appeared to offer some kind of scroll – only to be knocked into a heap by the intended recipient.

'You can observe a lot just by watching.'
– Yogi Berra (b. 1925), legendary New York Yankees player and coach

Though I was late for a meeting, my curiosity got the better of me, and when I reached the young man who had been running so hard, I asked him who the men were that he had wanted to meet. At that moment, his expression shifted from despair for himself, to astonishment, and then to pure pity for me and my obviously diminished mental capacity. 'What do you mean?,' he asked, incredulously. 'That was Madonna!'

He had hardly seen the men that formed Madonna's protective phalanx as he had tried to get his gift to his idol; I saw only the men and never noticed the woman running with them. Both of us saw what we expected and preferred. Though we were observers of the same events, what each of us brought to the scene was quite different, and so was what we took away.

Such slips of the perception are of relatively small import when they concern rock stars and offertory scrolls. But they can lead to major damage when they distort incoming data of all sorts – facts, figures, impressions, comments – and thereby derail the learning process related to a company's strategy and organization. Then, based on flawed observation, passage through the OODA Loop leads to consistently poor decisions, without the decision makers ever being clear on why options that looked so promising at the outset resulted in outcomes that were so disappointing.

Worse, this is a common result because all of us harbor implicit expectations and preferences that act as mental bodyguards, not unlike the material bodyguards running with the 'material girl.' If you want to increase the odds of seeing the data as they really are, a good first step is to take a look at the psychological mechanisms that underlie these perceptual filters – as well as at the business consequences that can ensue when we allow our expectations and preferences to operate unnoticed and therefore unchallenged.

Part one
Great expectations:
the efficiency of semi-automatic predictions

Expectations are predictions that have become semi-automatic, so much so that they have almost become part of the mental operating systems each of us uses to navigate through the world. Our lives are full of such semi-automatic but no longer very conscious predictions. They're useful because they allow us to make fast decisions on a whole gamut of subjects, from what to eat and what to wear, to how to succeed at love and at work.

In fact, it's difficult to envision what our lives would be like without such built-in expectations. Imagine what would happen if, every time you got into a car, you had to figure out what the brake did, how to use the accelerator, and why the manufacturers provided you with more than one gear; if every time you saw a traffic signal, you had to stop and think about what a green light means and how it differs from one that has turned red. Or, if every time you set about cooking breakfast, you had to grab a recipe book to determine how to cook an egg or make a proper pot of tea (although there is a wonderful scene of Bertie Wooster contemplating a kettle in one of the Jeeves stories by P. G. Wodehouse). Even the simplest of activities would take forever.

Or think back to when you joined a new company, were transferred to a different division, or otherwise found yourself in a new job with few bearings. Chances are that in the early stages, you felt disoriented and maybe even anxious. Eventually, to your great relief, the pieces began to come together. Then you could change the focus of your efforts from trying to figure out what was happening, to actually getting on with the work to be done, a shift made possible only because you had internalized a set of predictions that allowed you to make sense of your new environment, quickly and reliably. What seemed foreign initially had become second nature, allowing you to operate far more efficiently than you did initially.

And therein lies a vitally important power of expectations: to provide the 'economies of mind' that allow us to maneuver through a complex world with reasonable speed. Without them, we'd be overwhelmed by more incoming information than we could possibly process. But with them, we risk missing clues critical to *effective* behavior – that is, going where we want to go, rather than getting just any place fast. One source of this risk is to see what we expect to see, and not what we don't. A second is to see some discordant data – whether impressions or figures – but then beat them into submission so they confirm the existing story. And the third is to ignore sources that could disprove what we expect to be true. All are discussed in the remainder of this section. And all get in the way of learning.

Fogging the facts, part 1:
the optics of selective vision

In 1949, psychologists Jerome Bruner and Leo Postman published a study in the *Journal of Personality*. In that experiment, they projected a series of images of individual playing cards, with each card flashed on the screen for a very short amount of time. As the images flew by, the researchers asked the reviewers to describe what they saw. By and large, the responses were quite accurate. Except in one respect. That was because the researchers had slipped a *red* six of spades into the deck. The subjects, expecting hearts and diamonds to be red, and spades and clubs to be black, then 'saw' either a red six of *hearts* (rather than spades) or a *black* six of spades (rather than red). Their expectations had outweighed the facts. As a result, the respondents didn't see what was right in front of them. And what they did see wasn't what they had been shown.

'Facts are generally overesteemed. For most practical purposes, a thing is what men think it is.'

– John Updike
(b. 1932),
American
novelist

The Bruner–Postman experiment shows the power of expectations based on past experience to shape our perceptions. Our preexisting biases have the same power. That's what research conducted by Thomas Gilovich and Michael Frank, professors at Cornell University, shows. In one experiment, they tested biases related to uniform colors in professional sports by airing two videotapes of an aggressive American football scrimmage to groups of professionally trained referees. The videotapes were identical, except that in one the players wore black uniforms, and in the other, white ones. The result: 'The referees who saw the black-uniformed version rated the play as much more aggressive and deserving of a penalty than those who saw the white-uniformed version.' Once again, what was seen wasn't what was shown.

Misreading a playing card is no big deal. Similarly, there are probably more important things in life to worry about than whether your team got a penalty it didn't deserve or avoided one that it did. But in business, not seeing the signs that a new entrant is on the ascendant is a very big deal. So is misevaluating people and companies based on old biases. Now think about the last time you were surprised. In retrospect, were there any clues that you didn't see before the change that in retrospect seem more obvious?

Fogging the facts, part 2: the mechanics of data massage ... ... and other means of active distortion

Filtering out data that go against expectations is one way to maintain efficient mental operating systems. But sometimes we can't avoid seeing the data; they stare us in the face, or some pesky outsider keeps insisting that there's more to the story than we'd like to see. It's then that the second mechanism for fogging the facts comes into play: data massage. This is the sport of finding ways to rearrange the offending data so that they won't threaten the existing frame of reference, and therefore cannot have much of an impact on the decisions at hand.

One way to do this is simply to exile the data to 'not-relevant-to-us land.' Consider the car industry in the United States. By 1979, imports accounted for about 20 percent of the market. Yet well into the 1980s, US car makers calculated their market shares by dividing their sales into total sales for all *US* manufacturers. US steel makers did the same thing. It wasn't that executives in either industry weren't aware of the growing imports; by all accounts, they were. But in both industries the argument was that such imports were anomalies, that the vast bulk of the market would continue to buy American, and that therefore the only competitors that mattered were other US companies. The method of calculation excluded the potentially disruptive data from the frame of reference, and thereby ensured that the internal status quo would not be disturbed.

Another way to keep annoying data out of the frame of reference is to question their pedigree, by claiming that the methodologies used to collect and/or analyze them were flawed. That's good for placing the data in question in quarantine while the debate rages on about their validity or the collection is redone. In one company I know, the same research was redone six or so times over a ten year period, each time producing the same discomforting findings, and each time being discounted as the outcome of bad survey design (although of course the criticism always focused on a *new* flaw).

Some data, though, are less easy to push out of the frame of reference. Then the natural tendency is to beat them into submission, until they mean what you want them to mean. Maryann Keller, an equity analyst who follows the automotive companies, argues that as late as the mid-1980s, executives at Chevrolet interpreted their company's research as showing that people who bought imports did so only because they were snobs. Of all the interviews conducted in California, where the imports built their first market beachhead, the one retold most often reportedly was the young woman who said: 'If I had a blind date and he showed up in a Honda, I'd know we were going to a nice restaurant and then doing something fun afterwards. If he showed up in a Chevy, I'd figure that we were going to Jack in the Box.' The data that were remembered were the ones that supported a palatable storyline and thereby kept more unsettling interpretations at bay – such as the radical idea that Chevrolet needed to launch an all-out offensive in quality and design to win back its customers.

'There are no facts, only interpretation.'
– Friedrich Nietzsche (1844–1900)

Or consider the fashion company that was losing market share. Before I visited them, I went to stores to look at the product, and thought the styles were missing their target market by a mile. Later, when I met with the people from the company, I suggested that part of the problem might stem from the styling. No, I was told, this wasn't so, for the following reason: When this company ran focus groups, consumers had also told them that they thought the styles were unattractive. But then, when someone from the company entered the room and explained to participants why the items really weren't ugly, the participants 'understood' and changed their minds. As at Chevrolet, the facts were massaged to fit the preferred story.

Fogging the facts, part 3: Zen and the art of avoiding nonconfirming data

Here's another experiment to consider. Say I place four cards, face down, on a table in front of you. The back of the first card is marked with an 'A', the second with a '2', the third with a 'B', and the fourth with a '3'. Now suppose I ask you to determine whether 'all cards with a vowel on one side have an even number on the other.' And then suppose that I add the condition that you can only turn over two cards. Which two would you choose?

I'm somewhat embarrassed to report that when I saw this puzzle, I chose the one marked with the 'A,' and then the one with the '2.' As it turns out, in the original research, conducted in the 1960s, most respondents did the same. But while the card with the '2' can provide confirmation of the statement, it can't *prove* the statement. Now consider the card with the '3.' Though few people chose this card, it's the only one other than A that can disprove the statement. Table 6.1 shows how the choices map out.

The card experiment shows the effect of a theory on what data are collected, and for what purposes. Now think about the data collected by your company. How much is designed to provide confirmation (which may be read as 'proof'), and how much of it includes the search for information that can challenge the implicit logic being followed or perhaps reveal a new set of assumptions about your market, customers or products? And then imagine what the American auto industry might have looked

'The devil can cite scripture for his purpose.'
– William Shakespeare (1564–1616)

Table 6.1 Choices for the card experiment 'all cards with a vowel on one side have an even number on the other.' (Note: this statement does not say that cards with even numbers always have vowels, only that cards with vowels will have even numbers.)

Card	Provides confirmation (but not proof)	Disproves theory	Neither confirms nor disproves
A + even number	✓		
A + odd number		✓	
2 + consonant			✓
2 + vowel	✓		
3 + consonant			✓
3 + vowel		✓	
B + odd number			✓
B + even number			✓

like if, in the 1970s and early 1980s, it had considered the possibility that it was more than the snobbism of a few flaky Californians that was driving the market for imports. Not looking for data that can disprove your beliefs is risky business – and certainly limits how much you will learn, because you are unlikely to see what you do not look for.

Part two
Pride and preferences:
the emotion of seeing what you want to see

In some ways, preferences are expectations with an attitude. They work via similar mental mechanisms as expectations do, but now the ego kicks in, and with it a high level of emotions as well. If someone is insistent on presenting discordant data, you can prettily easily tell if it's an expectation or a preference that's being violated. In the case of a disrupted expectation, you'll probably feel vaguely discomfited and disoriented, and maybe a bit annoyed. But if it's a preference that's being tampered with, you'll likely feel a surge of emotion, a kind of 'how-dare-they?' feeling. You might punctuate your sentiments by turning red in the face, pounding on the table, or storming out of the room. Or you might steam quietly, while planning how to get the offender to learn better manners (preferably permanently).

I learned this first hand early in my consulting career when I was drawn onto a team to do a pricing analysis. The client was a small, venture-funded company in high-tech services, which I'll call 'The David Company.' David operated under the price umbrella of a major competitor that, naturally, I'll call 'Goliath Inc.' The smaller company was seeking another round of financing from its investors, and had based all its financial projections on the assumption that Goliath Inc. was going to increase prices by five percent plus inflation for the following year and then hold the prices even with inflation. After studying the market situation, however, I became convinced that Goliath's most likely action would be to *drop* its prices by at least five percent in real terms and then continue *lowering* prices at a less aggressive rate for the next five years, in order to protect its market position.

Such a price drop had enormous implications for The David Company, which would have to lower its prices too. This in turn would require cutting its costs. And cutting its costs would require a massive restructuring along with a complicated explanation to investors – both highly unpleasant tasks. So perhaps what transpired next was not surprising. Upon hearing the pricing predictions, the senior vice president of the smaller company treated me and the rest of the team to a classic example of reaction to a violated preference: he turned beet red, grabbed a felt-tip pen from the breast pocket of his jacket, slashed a large 'X' over the pricing data page, ripped the page out of the presentation book, rolled it into a ball, began yelling, and angrily declared the matter closed. (Despite my protests, the analysis was never presented again. But here's what did happen: Goliath Inc, unconcerned about this man's preferences, went ahead and did the 'inconceivable,' dropping its prices not by five percent but by ten, and which it then followed with more cuts each subsequent year. It is perhaps unnecessary to add that, in this tale, The David Company did not survive the battle with the Titan.)

'We can easily forgive a child who is afraid of the dark; the real tragedy of life is when men are afraid of the light.'
– Plato

There's a good reason for the kind of energy that all of us put into protecting our preferences. That's because our preferences are protecting what we see as being in our interests. Money is one such interest. But the two I see more commonly in the business context are comfort and pride.

The lust for comfort:
how not wanting to change can create voluntary blindness

Have you ever wondered why so many companies seem to be acting in a conscious and deliberate way to avoid seeing and acting on the information that's right in front of them – and right in front of everyone else? Just to list a few preeminent examples in the United States: IBM, Digital Equipment Company, Control Data, General Motors, Polaroid, and all the integrated steel makers – from Bethlehem to US Steel.

I used to think about such companies in terms of the analogy of the boiled frog. You know the one – put a frog in a beaker, turn the heat up high and the frog will jump out; but turn the heat up slowly and the frog will be boiled to death. The frog analogy says that if the increment of change is small enough, it becomes imperceptible, thus preventing remediative action. But not according to *Fast Company* magazine, whose experiments in the area suggest that the analogy is based on bad science, as in both cases the frog jumps out of the beaker, just as humans would do under similar circumstances. And frogs aside, I have become convinced that, beyond a certain point, when people in com-

panies persist in acting as though they can't see what's happening around them, something in addition to expectations is at
work. Often that something is the desire to maintain the comfort of the status quo.

In fact, it's hard to overestimate the role of comfort in motivating any of us to disregard data that imply nasty changes. Suddenly the world in which we operate is less predictable, leading
to feelings of anxiety and relative incompetence – sensations disliked by most of us, and especially disliked by senior executives
used to being in control (and who typically see both their status
and their compensation as based on their ability to stay in control). We may regard the changes as especially nasty if we find
that, for our companies to succeed, we have to cut back on doing
the stuff we like best – and, worse, that we have to start doing a
whole bunch of other stuff that we really don't like much, or
frankly aren't good at, or that we simply detest.

Let's go back to the American car industry. During the first
waves of the imported car invasions, it was probably the expectations of the executives sitting in Detroit that provided the initial
air cover for the Japanese companies. That's certainly what Yutaka
Katayama, Nissan's man in the US, was hoping for when he gave
this advice to colleagues working with him in the 1960s to crack
the US market: 'What we should do is get better and creep up
slowly, so we'll be good – and the customer will think we're good
– before Detroit even knows about us.'

If you're thinking that the US executives must have been stupid to have fallen into Katayama's trap, I invite you to try to
transport yourself back into the US landscape in the late 1950s
and early 1960s. The first Toyotas, introduced to the US in 1958,
were a joke. Toyota thought so too, yanked the cars, and then
stayed out of the market until 1964. The first Datsuns, produced
by Nissan and introduced at about the same time as the early
Toyotas, were just as bad, arriving in California with underpow-
ered engines, undersized batteries, and weak brakes. They also
had an involuntary climate-control system – the engine – that

made the cars so hot year-round that Datsun salesmen nicknamed them the 'mobile coffins.' Considering the circumstances, some Nissan staff speculated that company executives in Tokyo had selected 'Datsun' as the US moniker to protect the Nissan name in the likely case of failure. (The name for the North American market was finally changed to Nissan about twenty years later.)

But at some point, the preference to believe that the Japanese posed no real threat must have kicked in as well. Over time, Toyota, Nissan, and the other Japanese companies began to make obviously wonderful cars. If the executives sitting in Detroit had mapped their own products versus those of the intruders on the competitive-game maps shown in Chapter 3, and done so with even crude accuracy, they would have seen lower prices and higher benefits in every category except, perhaps, brand equity. But it wouldn't have taken a rocket scientist to predict that the reputations imputed to the Japanese name plates were soon going to soar as well, especially since, dollar for dollar, the Japanese cars were more comfortable, more reliable, and more attractive than the US alternatives.

Why was the preference to dismiss the Japanese so strong, especially given that the stakes were so high? I think it was because the status quo was so wonderfully comfortable. The competitors were few in number and close in proximity; the better to be able to anticipate each other's actions and move roughly in tandem. Customers were also roughly predictable, with car and model selection reflecting position in the social ladder, just as Alfred Sloan, the legendary CEO of General Motors, had theorized years before. This resulted in segments that were easy to address because they were defined primarily by demographics; Chevys for people at low end of the social spectrum, Caddies for those at the top. And the customers were docile; cars shimmied, stuttered, and fell apart with such regularity that people joked about planned obsolescence – but still kept buying the next models. In this world, managers could place their attention on the fun part of the business, the styling and launch of new models, and do the rest pretty much as they had the previous year. And they could do so in environments of great luxury, thanks to copious – and, I would say, excessive – executive perks, as later detailed in Maryann Keller's book on GM, *Rude Awakening*.

The moral of the story, though, has to do with consciousness, not cars. The more comfortable you are with the ways things work today, the more you have to be on the lookout for how your preferences to maintain this comfort is blocking your ability to see what's happening around you. And the more you find yourself yelling and fuming at people who bring you information that you think is wrong-headed and unpleasant, the more you need to reflect on how your own preferences are driving your perceptions and behavior.

> *'We do not see things as they are; we see things as we are.'*
> – The Talmud

The double-edge sword of pridefulness: how blindness due to pride can build and destroy companies

I think of preferences based on pride as being of two types. First are the ones based on pride with a little 'p.' These are the instances in which people hear only what pampers their egos, and angrily disregard that which does not. An example is the executive director of a trade association who heard a speech by two psychologists on the uses of upward feedback and, duly inspired, went back to his office, designed a confidential form, and circulated it to his staff. When things did not go exactly as he had preferred – because the employees were able to submit their answers anonymously and told him what they really thought – he simply had the forms reprinted and sent out again. But this time, he added a note, which said, 'I'd like you to fill out these forms again – and this time rate me accurately!'

It's the preferences based on pride with the big 'P' that are more interesting, because these are stuff that dreams are made of – and, more particularly, of visions that promise, and sometimes deliver, greatness. Consider Edwin Land, the founder of the Polaroid Corporation, and holder of more than 500 patents. From the time he started out in a dark basement apartment in New York, which he used as both his living quarters and his chemistry laboratory, through his founding and chairmanship of Polaroid, Land was guided by one principle: elegance of technology.

But the same pride that gave the world instant photography was also responsible for costly corporate blunders, because Land's response to information that violated his preferences was both swift and unpleasant. Take the focusing mechanism for Polaroid's breakthrough camera, the SX-70, introduced in 1972. Land's focusing system was the essence of elegance – the photographer simply turned the lens until the image seen through the viewfinder went from fuzzy to suddenly sharp. For people like Land with good vision, the device was perfect. But for those who were nearsighted or who wore bifocals or thick lenses, the shift could be impossible to detect.

Those critical of the focusing mechanism, however, had to brave Land's wrath. To the optical engineers who developed an alternative design, Land retorted that the consumers must be *taught* to use the viewfinder he had designed and insisted that the job of providing such instruction fell to the marketing department. When a half year later John Wolbarst, head of customer service at Polaroid and former editor of *Modern Photography*, used reports and transcripts from customer interviews to argue for the new focusing system, Land held to his original view. Even though the alternative viewfinder was finally accepted after yet another six months, it was said that Land never spoke to Wolbarst again.

'The great tragedy of science – the slaying of a beautiful hypothesis by an ugly fact.'
– Aldous Huxley

Land isn't an isolated example of the power of such pride; nor is this a North American phenomenon. Nissan's Katayama – the same guy who, as mentioned at the start of this book, used a screwdriver to get rid of the 'Fair Lady' nameplates on the sports car that came to be known as the Z – faced a continuing stream of similar problems with his superiors in Japan. That was because he insisted on sending Tokyo descriptions of requirements for competing in the US market that, as seen from Japan, seemed too improper to be considered seriously – and so, were not.

Nevertheless, Katayama persisted. Take his recommendation for more powerful engines. With their displacement of just 1000 cc, Nissan's export engines were even smaller than those used in the Volkswagen Beetle (1300 cc) and were almost laughable in comparison with the engines used in small US cars (5000 to 6000 cc). From the perspective of Tokyo, it was insulting to suggest that 1000 cc was insufficient; given the poor state of the Japanese road system at the time, it was difficult for a Nissan manager sitting in Tokyo to imagine that acceleration and engine power could really be that important to cracking the US market.

Or consider the very odd American desire to have cars with carpet mats attached to the floor. The Japanese, fastidious about cleaning their cars, liked removable carpet pads that could be readily shampooed and vacuumed; why would anyone fortunate enough to own their own car not do the same? Stranger still was the segment of American consumers who wanted trucks equipped with the amenities of passenger cars – softer suspensions, better upholstery, even air conditioning. In Japan, trucks were for hauling things, cars for transporting people. Why would anyone mix the two? More to the point, why would a company with any pride in its products create such a Frankenstein-ish vehicle? It took Katayama almost a decade, but he eventually convinced his bosses in Tokyo to look at products for the US market differently than their preferences would have led them. (Though this may seem to be an unconscionably long time, it was certainly faster than the time required by Nissan's counterparts in Detroit to deal with their respective expectations and preferences, suggesting that Katayama spent almost as much time trying to rouse his own management as he did trying keep his American competitors nestled in the arms of Morpheus. One doesn't need to go through the OODA Loop quickly by any absolute standard – just more quickly than one's competitors do.)

The kind of pride that both Land and the Nissan brass possessed illustrates the double-edged nature of such preferences. Pride, in fact, is the magic elixir of entrepreneurialism; it's what allows an Edwin Land, or a Bill Gates, or a Karl Benz, or a Soichino Honda or a Richard Branson to persevere despite all evidence to the contrary. When in retrospect such pride lines up with the right market forces, it's called vision; otherwise it seems more like delusion. But in either case, it does include a dose of pigheadedness that can make it impossible for individuals and groups to deal with unwelcome information. If you're certain that you fall into the category of those great leaders whose instincts and vision far outreach those of the people around you, this isn't a major problem. For the rest of us though, if we can't find ways to see our preferences and then test them, we run the risk that such filters will lead to decisions that are irrational at best – and deadly wrong at worst.

> *'A leader is someone who knows what they want to achieve and can communicate that.'*
> – Margaret Thatcher

Sense and sensibility: of focus and recognizing the yellow flags

'The humility to reexamine your certainties is the beginning of intelligence and innovation in any field.' That's the point of view taken by T George Harris, former editor-in-chief of *Psychology Today* and *The Harvard Business Review*. There's wisdom in this view – and also good empirical data to support it.

One example is another study led by Thomas Gilovich, in which the participants, who were told that the purpose was to test a student's belief in the prophetic nature of dreams, were given a copy of this student's diary – which, of course, had actually been written by the researchers. The diary had been constructed in the form of daily entries, each of which included the student's jottings on the dream she had the night before and the events of the current day. The diary was also constructed so that half the entries provided evidence confirming the student's belief in the prophetic nature of her dreams, and half the entries provided evidence contradicting it. Then the researchers added a twist by creating two versions of the diary. In the first version, given to half the participants, the student's dream from the previous night was always at the top of the entry, and the evidence – confirmatory or contradictory – was always at the end of the entry, marked off with the words, 'the most significant event of the day.' In the second version, given to the others, the dream was still at the top, but the evidence was buried some unpredictable place in the text.

Guess what happened. Participants who got the first version, the focused one, tended to remember about the same number of confirmatory and contradictory events, accurately reflecting the underlying data. Participants who got the second version, the unfocused one, showed a different pattern. Though they had been exposed to the same data, they tended to recall three times as many confirming events as contradictory ones.

Gilovich's findings demonstrate the need to identify core operating assumptions, as argued in the previous chapters of this book. But as expectations and preferences can clothe such assumptions in the appearance of self-evident truths, it's also important to be on the look-out for the warning signals of cognitive filters at work.

One kind of warning signal is the red flag. This is an easy signal to recognize as it typically starts with a red face. From there it can run to whatever it takes to repel the unwanted information: temper tantrums, tears, screamed rebuttals, *ad hominem* accusations, slammed doors, yelled obscenities and general histrionics – or, perhaps even more eloquently, frosty silence and withering looks. In some cases such reactions come from a passion for the issues at hand. In most, they are also, quite simply, displays of raw power – the means by which those whose preferences are being violated work to intimidate everyone else into silence. To this purpose, such power plays are often successful – at least in meeting the short-term wants of the protagonist – despite the very real risk they pose to the longer-term health of the organization. The key question then becomes whether the people whose preferences are being crossed have the discipline and integrity to permit a fuller discussion. When they do not, little can be done, other than by those more senior to them in the organization.

Then come what I think of as the 'yellow flags.' Though these warning signals take a bit more work to find than the more obvious red flags, they are also easier to deal with and then use as indicators of the need for more conscious attention and investigation. Here are three key ones.

Yellow flag #1: deflection and diffusion

If you've ever startled a covey of quail – at least the ones I've observed in the eastern US – you may have been treated to a fascinating display. The papa quail will shift, shuffle, dance, call out, and otherwise draw attention to himself. Meanwhile the mama quail and the babies will quietly sneak off to find cover. That behavior is hard wired into the birds, and sometimes I think it is in humans too – though we are infinitely more creative in the ways we deflect and diffuse attention from topics we don't want to address.

First, of course, comes all manner of body language that signals discomfort. Shifting in chairs. Ear tugging and other fidgeting. A sudden desire to straighten a picture frame, reprogram an electronic organizer, check e-mail, or adjust a light fixture. Then come the more obvious clues; nervous laughter or sharp jokes that diffuse tension – and deflect attention. And the most overt of all, changing the topic, often by declaring that time is up, or a rushed consensus based on a cobbled compromise – anything to avoid confronting anxiety-producing topics. (Agendas with time limits, often included as part of a TQM program, provide a wonderful excuse for those wishing to avoid troublesome topics. All the moderator has to say is, 'Right. That was our 23 minutes for item #6' – and it's onto the next item, regardless of relative importance.)

The best way I know out of this dilemma is simply to face it straight on, by identifying the underlying preferences that are being challenged and the alternate views. And this requires tolerance for dissonance and ambiguity – and the time to tackle the issues thoughtfully, both for discussion as well as further investigation.

Yellow flag #2: edge embroidery

Imagine the *Mona Lisa* without the woman in the center of the painting, *Whistler's Mother* without Ma, or even Gustav Klimt's *The Kiss* without the couple. The backgrounds may be lovely, but presumably, you'd feel that something was missing. But before you dismiss this as a ridiculous analogy, consider what happens in many companies. As evidence builds that something has to change, the core issues – which are tough to deal with – remain untouched, while an enormous number of peripheral efforts get launched as if, once again, being busy were the same as being productive. GM during the 1980s provides a perfect example; consultants were brought in by the truckload, acquisitions were made one after another, and automation and robots became a company mania. Everything, it seems, was being revisited, rethought, and restructured – everything, that is, except the core issue of designing and manufacturing substantially better cars at reasonable prices. I've seen a number of organizations respond to similar situations in the same way: urgent activity on subsidiary issues; little attention to the core.

'Wherever you see a successful business, someone once made a courageous decision.'
– Peter Drucker

Is this happening in your company? One way to find out is to make a list of the three to five issues you think are most critical to the future of your organization. Then look at where ninety percent of the effort is going. How much is dedicated to embroidery around the edges, and how much to mission-critical matters?

Yellow flag #3: going to Vegas

It has been said that in the early days of Federal Express, when the company had run out of money, founder Fred Smith did two things. He instructed his people to hide the company's aircraft from creditors seeking to repossess them. And he scrabbled some money together from kith and kin, flew to Las Vegas, and placed some humungous bets. Fortunately for Federal Express, both tactics worked, despite the size of the assets to be hidden and the odds against the wagers.

Though this story is remarkable, many companies develop strategies that are the functional equivalents of going to Vegas and putting every chip on 32 Red. They do this by developing plans that they claim to be realistic and hard-nosed, but that in fact are highly optimistic; the equivalent of GM believing in 1980 that, for some reason, sales of imported vehicles would not continue to grow. And, as at the tables in Vegas, the only thing worse than putting all your money on 32 Red and knowing it, is putting all your money on 32 Red and not knowing it because you've comforted yourself with the illusion that you've just placed your cash in a conservative, well-managed investment portfolio.

To get a clearer bead on whether your organization has gone to Vegas, compare the base case of the strategy with the best case. The closer these two cases are, the more likely it is that you are operating on the basis of the most optimistic option – the strategic equivalent of betting on 32 Red. Then, if you're willing to heed this warning sign, you'll be more aware of the degree to which your preferences are at work – which in turn will lead you to a choice: to pursue the strategy on faith or to reevaluate the key assumptions on which it is based. There are successful examples of both; only you can decide which holds better odds for your organization.

Missing Madonna in a sea of bodyguards affects only a few
people and not very much. Missing a major market move
affects many, and quite substantially. The tragedy is that
often the data were there for the seeing, but were still
ignored or distorted. And that's the paradox of the learning organization: many people espouse it, but fewer are
willing to endure the discomfort of learning, which always starts with the possibility that one's own most cherished expectations and preferences might turn out to be
inappropriate, incorrect, or just flat out insane.

'To see what is in front of one's nose requires a constant struggle.'
– George Orwell

• • •

One of the saddest business documents I have ever read is the
testimony given before the Rogers Commission, the group formed
to investigate the tragedy of the space shuttle Challenger. As you
may remember, Challenger was launched on January 28, 1986,
with a crew of seven including one civilian, Christa McAuliffe, a
young mother and school teacher from New Hampshire. As the
nation watched in horror, just after liftoff, the booster rocket
blew up, instantly killing the entire crew.

As the Rogers Commission did its work, the technical facts of
the matter came clear. The day of the launch was abnormally cold
for Florida, which affected the O-rings and joint seals in the solid
rocket booster. When the O-rings and joint seals then failed in
flight, the booster rocket exploded.

This result should not have been a total surprise. The engineers
and managers at Morton Thiokol, maker of the booster rocket,
and officials at NASA, Thiokol's customer, were aware of data that
suggested an increased risk of O-ring malfunction at temperatures below 53 degrees Fahrenheit. Still, they let the launch proceed. Why? At one level, the Commission's conclusions provide
the answer: 'Thiokol management reversed its position and recommended the launch of 51-L … in order to accommodate a major customer.'

Then the question becomes why, given dedicated and talented professionals, this reversal took place. Here the testimony before the Commission about the pre-launch decision process for Challenger is particularly poignant. As the testimony showed, the Thiokol team recommended *against* a launch, given the cold temperatures. But then representatives of NASA – Thiokol's customer – made their displeasure clear: one remarked that he was 'appalled,' another expressed his dismay that a launch might be delayed until April, three months away. And that in turn started a chain reaction, culminating in a discussion in which the Thiokol team of managers and engineers withdrew to discuss the problem without the participation of NASA personnel. As the Thiokol group leaned toward reversing its no-go recommendation, two of the engineers tried desperately to have the original recommendation upheld. In testimony to the Rogers Commission, Roger Boisjoly, one of the engineers, described what happened next:

> *Those of us who opposed the launch continued to speak out … And we were attempting to go back and re-review and try to make clear what we were trying to get across, and we couldn't understand why it was going to be reversed. So we spoke out and tried to explain once again the effects of low temperature. Arnie [Arnold Thompson, one of the other Thiokol engineers] actually got up from his position which was down the table and walked up the table and put a quarter pad down in front of the table, in front of the management folks, and tried to sketch out once again what his concern was with the [nozzle] joint, and when he realized he wasn't getting through, he just stopped.*
>
> *I tried one more time with the photos. I grabbed the photos and I went up and discussed the photos once again and tried to make the point that it was my opinion from actual observations that temperature was indeed a discriminator and we should not ignore the physical evidence we had ob-*

served ... I also stopped when it was apparent that I couldn't get anybody to listen ...

I really did all that I could to stop the launch ...

The process was very subtle, and it was only afterward that one of the pivotal participants, Jerry Lund, Thiokol's manager of engineering, realized that the usual standards for a launch had shifted – the burden of proof had shifted from justifying a launch to justifying a delay. The combination of expectations and preferences, though subtle, proved deadly.

The lesson from Challenger, though more tragic, is the same as the lesson from the other stories in this chapter. All of us can act only on the facts we see. Which facts we see depends on how much effort we're willing to invest and how much anxiety we're willing to endure. Make no mistake, however. Ignoring or distorting the facts doesn't make them go away – it just makes us less prepared to deal with the consequences they can cause.

Forward Intelligence System

There are only two ways of telling the complete truth –
anonymously … and posthumously.

– Thomas Sowell

Signs when your intelligence systems look forward ...
... but you still keep falling back in the battles that count

- The way your company deals with incoming intelligence provides proof positive of black holes as predicted by Einstein's General Theory of Relativity – information comes in, but is never seen or used again.

- Executives in your company are managing by all the latest theories, yet none of the techniques seems to be working like the books promised:

    ◦ Open-door policies are the norm, but few walk in

    ◦ Execs manage by walking around, but always seem to hear the same canned story every time they drop by

    ◦ Suggestion boxes have been placed in strategic locales, but the biggest harvest to date was three candy wrappers, a bad joke, and one anatomically impossible suggestion for what management could do to itself.

The management team has therefore concluded that there is little information to be retrieved, other than what they already know.

- When told to 'speak frankly,' subordinates joke about 'CLMs' – career limiting moves. Top management can never figure out the source of the concern, as the information offered hardly ever seems shocking or otherwise out of line.

- People who rock the boat with disruptive information can expect swift managerial response, usually in the form of being tagged with one of the following labels:

  - 'disloyal' (and therefore not to be trusted)

  - 'poor team player' (and therefore not to be trusted)

  - 'maverick' (and therefore not to be trusted)

  - 'not very bright' (and probably a poor hire in the first instance)

  - all of the above.

- The effective definition of teamwork has become: doing what the leader wants, cheerfully.

- People in top management positions often complain that they're the last to know about important developments, especially when the news is bad.

- Somehow, even when the pertinent information was available internally, other organizations seem to get the jump in the marketplace, giving new relevance to the expression, 'a day late and a dollar short.'

On 17 September 1862, the turning point of the American Civil War took place: the great Battle of Antietam, fought to a draw along the Antietam creek in western Maryland. Prior to this battle, the South, under the command of General Robert E. Lee, was poised for military and diplomatic victory. On the military side, Lee's forces had gained the upper hand in virtually every aspect of the conflict, and were now successfully pressing their campaign to invade the North. On the diplomatic side, Britain was about to extend diplomatic recognition, 'which,' in the view of Civil War historian Bruce Catton, 'as things stood then, would almost automatically have meant Southern independence.'

That the South did not prevail decisively at Antietam was the consequence of a string of events that began with an accident: a Confederate officer lost a copy of the battle masterplan, handwritten by Lee's assistant adjunct general. Then good fortune and good judgment combined to aid the Union cause. First, two enlisted Union soldiers found what later came to be known as 'the Lost Order' and, in one of the more spectacular examples of how decisions of people at the bottom of the pyramid can change history, made it their business to get the serendipitous treasure to George B. McClellan, General of the Union forces. Second, among McClellan's staff was an officer who could authenticate the handwriting as that of Lee's assistant adjunct general, and thereby convince McClellan that the found document was what it appeared to be.

That the North did not prevail decisively in this battle was the consequence of a failure of command. The plans revealed that Lee had dangerously divided his forces, which meant that McClellan and his forces at Antietam were now closer to each of the several pieces of the Confederate army than these pieces were to each other. 'Now,' comments Catton, 'McClellan had the game in his hands ... If he moved fast, McClellan could destroy the [Confederate] Army of Northern Virginia' and thereby end the war.

'That's the way it
is in war. You
win or lose, live
or die – and the
difference is just
an eyelash.'
– General
Douglas
MacArthur
(1880–1964),
World War II
hero

Instead, McClellan hesitated, allowing the portions of the Confederate army to reconnect and remass. Though the Battle of Antietam effectively put an end to the South's invasion plan and, with it, the immediate threat of diplomatic recognition for the Confederacy, the costs were great. One was the casualty count from the battle itself; 12,000 men lost for the North and almost as many for the South, in what was the become the single bloodiest day of the Civil War. The other was the escalating carnage as the war raged on for another thirty-two months.

How could the North have scored one of the most important intelligence coups in history and then allowed the treasure to lose much of its potential value? Some have hypothesized that McClellan was more worried about not losing than winning, and therefore moved too cautiously; certainly the General was known to be very deliberate in style. More recently, another interpretation has emerged, this one from the military analyst in charge of the US Central Intelligence Agency's 'staff rides' – walking tours of historic battlefields to help CIA personnel deepen their understanding of ground combat. His theory, as subsequently reported in the *Los Angeles Times*: the real problem lay more in the North's intelligence system than in the personality of one man.

The CIA analysis starts with the fact that the position of Union troops just prior to this battle had blocked Lee's ability to communicate with Confederate headquarters in Richmond, Virginia. In consequence, Lee had to make his own decisions, and quickly. McClellan, however, faced no such barrier and therefore the first action he took when he arrived at Antietam was to establish a telegraph line back to the War Department in Washington. That was the correct thing to do, at least according to the military procedures of the day. But it also added time to the decision-making process; time to relay the messages, time for the officials in Washington to assimilate the information and form their views, time to engage in debate. The analyst's conclusion? 'Lee was lucky. He was cut off from Richmond.' In this case, speed in using available but incomplete information was at least as valuable as having perfect information but moving slowly to capitalize on it.

Fast forward to today's business world and you're unlikely to find many people who don't understand the need for rapid and accurate corporate intelligence in all its variations – information, impressions, intuitions, and ideas – and who wouldn't rejoice at their companies snagging an intelligence windfall comparable to McClellan's. After all, one has to assume that competitors are always devising schemes for creating new markets or taking share; that's a basic of business life. Similarly, we all recognize that customer and employee needs are going to change, whether we want them to or not. As a result, just about every organization makes some kind of investment in gathering advance intelligence from and about key groups – including employees, suppliers, customers, competitors, and regulators – and believes that these efforts provide at least a step in the right direction.

Despite these good intentions, though, many companies find that they derive little return from their intelligence investments in formal systems, targeted research, and consultants' reports. Two kinds of organizational obstacles account for much of the disappointment. One is composed of those conditions and caveats that lead people who have useful ideas and intelligence to choose to withhold them, thereby constricting the volume of contributions at their sources. The other is made up of those systems and structures that have become unnecessary information dikes and dams, dangerously reducing the speed at which any new intelligence moves through the organization from input to action. Both can turn great intentions into substandard intelligence.

> *'Arguably, a wonderful case could be made in defense of corporate anarchy. Wonderful things can happen when a company's executives are so preoccupied by corporate infighting that they can't mess around too much with the movies [– or other products –] gliding off their assembly line.'*
> – Variety Editor-in-Chief Peter Bart, on the movie biz

Part one
The law of large numbers:
no WIF-MEs for me, no info for you

'The future has a
way of arriving
unannounced.'
– George F. Will,
American
columnist

Business is full of cruel surprises. Competitors come up with better deals than your company offers and launch them before you know what hit you. Customer hot buttons shift while your organization ponies up continued investments based on an outdated understandings of the market, thereby guaranteeing results that will fall far short of expectations. Employees are unhappy or are dodging the rules, and top management remains clueless about the problem until the resulting damage becomes obvious. All these surprises are costly; that's almost always clear, at least in retrospect. But here's the pity: in the vast majority of cases I've observed, most of the data about the impending danger or possible opportunity were either already resident somewhere within the organization, or could have been obtained fairly easily. And worse: in most cases, the lion's share of the blame for not getting the information to the right people at the right time falls not at the feet of those who chose not to share what they knew, but rather at the other end of the transaction – with the people who *needed* the information rather than those who had it.

Many managers feel either perturbed or baffled when confronted by such a claim. They see the flow of information, intelligence, intuition, and ideas as a partnership between the company and its customers, suppliers and employees. Accordingly, in this view, if anyone in any of these groups has useful information, it's the obligation of that party to offer up the goods while there's still time to make the changes that will avoid a pitfall or capture an opportunity. But while this belief is quite widespread, it violates what we might call 'The First Law of Intelligent Intelligence Systems,' which goes like this:

a.   *all other things being equal, a large number of contributions to the information flow is better than a small number;*

b.   *the number of contributions volunteered to any organization is directly related to the degree to which the info-holders perceive the likely rewards of making the contribution as exceeding the likely costs.*

In other words, people won't speak up unless there's something in it for them – the information version of the WIF-MEs (*what's-in-it-for-me*s) introduced in Chapter 5, and now applied to those with intelligence to contribute. Figure 7.1 shows the implicit arithmetic from the info-holders' point of view.

Starting point: my intrinsic desire to add to the info flow
  −   the likely penny-ante costs and hassles of making my contribution
  −   probability I assign to: incurring catastrophic personal costs
  +   probability I assign to: gaining rewards I care about

equals: likelihood I will offer my ideas, information, impressions and intuitions

Fig. 7.1   The info-holder's basic arithmetic.

As shown in Fig. 7.1, the starting point for this calculation is each individual's inclination to collect the stuff that good intelligence systems depend on – to note impressions and indiscretions, have ideas and inspirations, think up initiatives and imagine solutions – and then to derive satisfaction from sharing the items they've collected. Some people just can't help themselves when it comes to adding to the information flow; they're always noticing things, wondering why events occur as they do, and considering what might make them work better. Others notice little, and share less.

For the former group, which is probably the minority, it doesn't take much to prime the information pump, and sometimes even dire penalties won't shut it off. For everyone else, though, the three other factors noted in Fig. 7.1 – the penny-ante costs, perceived risk of catastrophic losses, and probability of meaningful rewards – are most important in shaping what is noticed and determining whether and with whom these treasures will be shared. And it's these three factors that provide the basis for the discussion in the rest of this section.

Factor #1: penny-wise and pound-foolish – the hidden costs of the hassle factor

Not long ago, I was on a one-stop flight on an airline that shall remain nameless. The flight was scheduled to go from Phoenix to Chicago to Boston, all on the same plane with the same crew. The flight didn't go quite as planned, however, because Chicago was fogged in and, after seemingly interminable circling, we were finally rerouted to Louisville, Kentucky. There, as the plane was being refueled, I gleaned the following information from a variety of sources: our flight crew was Chicago-based; we were being refueled for another go at landing in Chicago; our crew was over its work time and so would be released when we landed; and that while we might be able to land in Chicago, no flights would be leaving from that airport for the remainder of the evening. One other detail: the flight crew had already been notified that we passengers were *not* going to be given hotel vouchers for the night once we were finally deposited at the Chicago airport. Armed with these info-bits, I asked to be allowed off the plane before it continued on its appointed course. Once inside the terminal at Louisville, I met Lois Lane – not the Lois Lane of Superman fame but a real Lois Lane – in this case, a gate agent for US Air, the airline I switched to in order to get home.

'There is a time for departure even when there's no certain place to go.'
– Tennessee Williams (1911–1983), American playwright

I had two encounters with the fabulous Lois Lane. The first occurred when I arrived at the gate to purchase my tickets for my new flights (Louisville to Baltimore; then Baltimore to Boston).

Then, certain that my transaction was complete, I went to a payphone to make some business calls. Meanwhile, it seems the passengers on my previous flight mounted a rebellion and thereby compelled Airline X to let everyone off the aircraft and provide them with the paperwork for transfering to other carriers at no charge. But, knowing nothing about that event, I arrived back at the gate for my new flight to Baltimore with little time to spare – and no refund form. No problem, Ms. Lane assured me and, in true Superwoman fashion, moved faster than a speeding bullet to complete the following tasks: arranged to make sure the plane wouldn't take off without me, planted me at the door of the jetway, took my ticket, ran the length of the airport to Airline X's counter, extracted the appropriate paperwork, ran back, put through a refund for my earlier ticket purchase, and hustled me onto the plane (which left at its scheduled time, thanks to the alacrity with which gate agent Lane accomplished these tasks).

Before I met Lois Lane, US Air was tops on my list of least favorite airlines, and none of the ads the company ran had ever made an iota of difference in my attitude; now I am routinely impressed by the airline's workforce, especially its gates agents and flight attendants. But despite how Lois Lane changed my perspective, I never sang her praises to the US Air brass. Not that I didn't try; I asked numerous gate agents and flight attendants for either a comment form or the address of whom I should write to provide a compliment. Of the six I asked, five told me that they had no idea and the sixth give me a tiny scrap of yellowed fac-simile paper on which was printed a mail box number to which complaints could be sent.

Of course, I could have taken the time to get the CEO's name and address, and then written a formal letter. But that's just the point: if you create enough hassle and penny-ante costs, impor-tant contributions to the organization's information flow will be withheld. Two losses then ensue. One is loss of data about what and who is working well, which can help in figuring which systems and products should be maintained or expanded, and which people should be commended and rewarded. The other is loss of data about what and who is working poorly; all those irritating complaints and protests, justified and not, that can drive a management team mad – and that also don't go away simply because you've figured out a way to keep cross words from crossing your desk. Quite the contrary, when a company makes it difficult for small concerns to get to the right eyes and ears, either the complaints fester or the complainers find other, more receptive audiences – including customers the company is trying to woo, employees it's trying to motivate, competitors it's trying to outdo, or regulators it's trying to placate.

Has your company made penny-ante costs a regular part of the information-flow equation? Here are some common signs:

- You provide customers and employees with an outlet for ideas or concerns … an address. Your rationale is that if these people care that much, they can take the time to write a letter, address the envelope, and find a stamp.

'All the beautiful sentiments in the world weigh less than a single lovely action.'
– James Russell Lowell (1819–1891), American poet, essayist, and playwright

- You've put an employee idea program in place … which requires figuring out all the details for implementation, filling out forms or writing memos, and then waiting months for a response.

- You've set up toll-free numbers for customer comments and complaints … but the lines are often busy, or ring multiple times before being answered, or require callers to wend their way through a tortuous voice mail labyrinth, or result in callers being put on hold for long periods of time, or most or all of the above.

These aren't the only ways to impose penny-ante costs on those with information and ideas to contribute, of course; organizations are infinitely creative in creating hassles for others while optimizing for their own convenience and attempting to keep their own operations running smoothly, at least in the short run. None-theless, seemingly trivial costs can make the difference between information volunteered and information withheld, especially when it's easier for the information holder to switch off rather than speak up. Then any but the most trivial expense will be the obstacle to speaking up.

Sound farfetched? Think of the times you've been irritated or pleased either as a customer or as an employee the past year or even the past month. Of these, in how many cases did you make the effort to give the pertinent information to the right people in the format as required by their organization? (If your number was somewhere south of ten percent, your personal results reflect what studies of customer dissatisfaction typically show: many are vexed, but few are verbal – at least, not through the formal channels that they're 'supposed' to use.)

Or consider what happens inside companies, especially when management decides that the ticket-to-play for making sugges-tions is presenting ideas the way senior managers do: in formal, well crafted memos, written in proper business language with good grammar and correct spelling. Richard Feynman saw these effects first hand when, as a member of the Rogers Commission investigating the Challenger Shuttle disaster, he looked into why the solid rocket boosters in NASA space shuttles became a little out of round after each use. Having been told by the manager of the area that the problem was due to mistakes by the workers in the solid rocket booster assembly area, Feynman went to talk with the workers themselves. Here's what he found:

> *Mr Lamberth [the manager of the area] didn't really know what happened ... [because] he never talked to them [the work-ers] directly... They had noticed all kinds of problems and had all kinds of ideas on how to fix them, but no one had paid much attention to them. The reason was: Any observations had to be reported in writing and a lot of these guys didn't know how to write good memos.*

In fact, as Feynman subsequently discovered, the root cause of the defects wasn't the workers at all, but the procedures manual, which contained incorrect instructions. The workers in the booster area saw the problems and had figured out solutions – but simply found it too costly, in terms of time and energy, to try to communicate their ideas to those higher up in the organization. Many employee idea programs suffer a similar fate due to requirements that seem reasonable to management – for example, that all ideas have to be accompanied by an actionable implementation plan – but overwhelming to the employees. Then, as with the solid rocket boosters, the penny-ante costs effectively shut down the flow of information and intelligence.

People who claim that their employees and suppliers should be loyal enough to go through a few hoops to put their ideas in proper business format, or that any customer with an issue worth hearing about shouldn't mind having to make a little extra effort, have missed the point. Getting the information you need isn't about shoulds; it's about getting the information. Period.

Factor 2: disloyalty tests and teamwork traps – the risk of committing a CLM (career-limiting move)

Few costs in the information-flow equation are more underestimated than those related to the perceived likelihood of adverse outcomes: the risk of transmitting important information and then being handed your head for doing so. The reason for the gross underestimation has to do with the gap in power between those who have something to say but are subordinate and those who might not want to hear it but have the ability to control conditions and careers.

From the point of view of the people in the dominant power position, the situation is clear: if I go fifty percent of the way and have an open door policy, manage by walking around, conduct surveys, and invest in idea programs, then you need to go fifty percent of the way and speak your mind. But when it comes to information flows, the idea of a 50–50 split in responsibility is total nonsense, unless the power is split 50–50 as well. Otherwise, the person in the subordinate power position has to consider the risk that speaking out will result in bad things coming back on the return trip; a reduction in orders for a supplier, a change in service levels for a customer, or a one-way ticket to career Siberia for an employee. If this risk is perceived to be more than minuscule, then you can count on a great many ideas, initiatives, impressions, and other forms of intelligence remaining unexpressed.

Sometimes the people seeking the information sidestep this problem by telegraphing the answer they wish to receive in advance. My favorite example of how this mechanism works comes from a set of letters that Lewis Carroll sent to thirty mothers of young children seeking advice about an illustration that had been submitted as the frontispiece for *Through the Looking Glass* and with which Carroll was unhappy. Here's what the letter said:

> *I am sending you, with this, a print of the proposed frontispiece for* Through the Looking-glass. *It has been suggested to me that it is too terrible a monster, and likely to alarm nervous and imaginative children; and that at any rate we had better begin the book with a pleasanter subject.*
>
> *So I am submitting the question to a number of friends, for which purpose I have had copies of the frontispiece printed off.*
>
> *We have three courses open to us:*
>
> (1) *To retain it as the frontispiece.*
>
> (2) *To transfer it to its proper place in the book (where the ballad occurs which it is intended to illustrate) and substitute a new frontispiece.*
>
> (3) *To omit it altogether.*

'To consult is to seek another's advice on a course already decided upon.'
– Ambrose Bierce (1842–1914), American humorist and author of the original *Devil's Dictionary*

The last named course would be a great sacrifice of the time and trouble which the picture cost, and it would be a pity to adopt it unless it is really necessary.

I should be grateful to have your opinion (tested by exhibiting the picture to any children you think fit) as to which of these courses is best.

It should come as no surprise that the answer returned was option 2. Of course, Lewis Carroll didn't hold real power over the mothers whom he polled, other than gravitational force of politeness; who wants to rock a well-structured social situation by appearing to be rude? But now consider the corporate analogue: market research. If the market research department is funded at the behest of top management, why wouldn't one anticipate that in many companies, much of the research will be designed to produce the answers expected and preferred by those who control the budget for the department? The bias may be subliminal, subtle, or even unintentional, but no less influential in shaping the how research is designed, the results achieved, and the way the reports are written.

'When companies do their own surveying, they tend to get the answers they want, accurate or not.'
– Richard G. Hamermesh, author, Fad-Free Management

Feedback of a more direct type is provided when people who try to tell the truth get ignored or, worse, hurt in the process; identified as bad actors, poor team players, malcontents, or just plain disloyal. They then also become the examples that others use to estimate the risks of speaking up. Harvey Gittler, vice president of operations for a division of a US-based manufacturing company, could be the poster boy for such risks. His saga began when top corporate executives blew into town to review the division's performance and plans and the usual dog-and-pony show ensued. The head of engineering, rhapsodized about the new product line … without mentioning the continuing reliability problems. The head of marketing effervesced about the tremendous customer response … while failing to report that product returns were almost equal to shipments. And the head of sales pointed enthusiastically to the projected future growth in revenues ... leaving out the fact that all the data collected thus far suggested that the forecasts were grossly overstated.

As Gittler tells the story, aware that the division would have to deal with the realities of defective products, growing piles of un-sold inventory, and unrealistic sales forecasts, he decided to give the straight story about manufacturing when the spotlight came to him. His reward? An admonishment from his boss to 'change his attitude,' followed by a handwritten note from his boss's boss at corporate that said, 'I really can't understand your present sense of anxiety. You have a manufacturing guy's dream – a sold-out plant; a need to scale up production; a hungry, worldwide sales organization; a supportive relationship with engineering.'

Gittler drew this conclusion: 'There is a limit to how much one can speak out, regardless of the facts ... No one, especially the brass, wants to hear the truth in those settings. That's why, in my next job, I did not repeat my mistake. I told it the way 'they' wanted to hear it.'

Is your organization falling into the swamp of complicit silences; the illusion of an open environment and the reality of censored information? One warning sign is if those at the top hardly ever hear unpleasant or unexpected information, or are typically among the last to know about developing problems.

According to Sergei Kondrashev, the ex-KGB agent who used to run the KGB's German operations, that was exactly the state of affairs that Stalin created when he ruled the Soviet Union. No country had better intelligence operations. But though KGB spies beat all in collecting superbly accurate information, the agents were also mindful that those who told Stalin what he didn't want to hear literally faced having their heads handed to them or, if they were luckier, finding their careers suddenly jammed into full-speed reverse. In consequence, they converted accurate informa-tion into palatable information, which in turn led Stalin to make costly blunders in a range of foreign hot spots, from Berlin to Korea. The moral of the story applies to companies as well as countries: the world is changing fast enough that the lack of bad news can itself be an indicator of censored or blocked information, no matter how great the underlying intelligence-gathering system.

Another warning sign is if bad news is offered and then shooed away, like some unwanted garden pest. Here are a few common information-swatters:

- 'What could you have been thinking? You clearly don't know what you're talking about! I thought you had a better understanding of our business than that!'

- 'I'm quite surprised to hear you say these things! And disappointed. This is a time when we all have to pull together to get the job done!'

- 'What a minute, whose side are you on, anyway? We like team players around here, you know.'

- 'Hey, look everybody! We've got an anarchist in our midst! Got any other insurrections you'd like to foment?'

- 'Oh, stop with the excuses, already. We take a can-do attitude around here. So quit your belly aching and get back to work.'

- 'That's a great insight. But, you know, your performance review is coming up. Perhaps you should wait until after that before you say anything.'

- 'Why are you always so negative?'

'I am sitting in the smallest room in the house. I have your review in front of me. Soon it will be behind me.'
– Max Reger (1873–1916)

Reactions like these, whether accompanied by grins or grimaces, send powerful messages. They telegraph to all that the information giver may be about to or may already have committed a 'CLM' – a career-limiting move. And they imply serious criticisms: that the information is badly flawed, indicating that the giver is not so bright; or that the giver, though competent, has questionable loyalties or abilities as a team player. Embedded in all of them are the real catastrophic losses that people fear: the risk of burning up goodwill and its associated advantages, including promotions, assignments, and compensation, as well as the various other goodies that the listeners control.

They also just about guarantee that the organization will suffer additional losses. True loyalty and teamwork require the ability to engage in vigorous debate, even confrontation, when needed; dissent from the heart is the ultimate act of allegiance. Yet many managers routinely conduct loyalty tests that send clear messages to potential contrarians, or use the goal of frictionless teamwork to regulate who can speak up and what they can say. The dilemma is all the more difficult because many people are not very skilled at expressing their concerns gracefully or constructively, and therefore come across as disruptive or hostile even when their intentions are good and their news is important. But one thing is clear: if the perceived risks of speaking up are high, the information flow will be constricted at its sources, no matter how many new approaches mangers try, or how much they manage by walking around, or how open they proclaim their doors to be.

Factor #3: the physics of honey – the probability of gaining rewards for volunteering information

It's an old saying in the southern US that one can catch more flies with honey than with vinegar. You might question why anyone would want to catch flies. One answer is that what works with insects can work with ideas and information, too – but only for those organizations willing to provide rewards that matter to the people with the information.

What kinds of rewards? The obvious one is money. Customers who participate in market-research projects are often paid for their time. Employees can be awarded a portion of the savings or profits that result from their input in the form of cash bonuses or other prizes. And suppliers who offer good ideas and other information to their customers are often rewarded for their efforts with increased orders or a bit more in margin.

But make no mistake: despite the impact that money can have, extra financial incentives are often not sufficient, and sometimes not even necessary, to keep the volume of ideas and information flowing to and through an organization. Instead, in many cases, the most valuable reward, with or without a financial sweetener, is action – anything from thoughtful acknowledgment to the ultimate prize of turning input into reality. And while 'action' may sound like the easiest and least expensive reward to provide, in practice it's the one most often withheld, with invisible but indelible effects on the kind and volume of intelligence that will be offered in the future.

Consider a few examples. For customers, filling out a questionnaire or attending a focus group takes time. For many, a token monetary payment no longer suffices; the quid pro quo now is the courtesy of well designed research (easy to complete, focused on the right issues), plus commitment to making the indicated changes. In this sense, every market research foray becomes a contract; if I do you the favor of supplying the information you've requested, you need to do me the courtesy of considering the findings seriously and then acting on them in a timely and intelligent way. Otherwise, count on me to toss all your subsequent requests and inquiries into the trash bin.

For employees too, the reward of action is often withheld as companies ask for suggestions, mark the appropriate check-box on some list of 'managerial imperatives,' and then provide no evidence of consciousness at the receiving end. That's why many attempts to implement great sounding programs – periodic town meetings, management by walking-around, brown-bag lunches for the rank and file with members of top management, and the like – end up flopping; lots of ritualized discussion, but no real dialogue.

That's also why many companies find that their requests for suggestions and information backfire. In fact, asking without acting is worse than not asking at all, leading to increased cynicism and an accompanying reduction in the kinds and amount of intelligence offered. Take the company that conducted an employee satisfaction survey, found that the top complaint was the sorry state of the cafeteria, published the results, and then ... did nothing. Said one manager, 'Before, we could kid ourselves that the bosses did not know how bad the cafeteria was. After the survey, we knew they just didn't care.'

Or consider the chemist who was asked to help redesign the sample compositing room in which he worked. He and his colleagues agreed that a sloped floor to the drain was the most important feature to be included in the renovation because then they could hose down all the raw materials quickly and efficiently. Excited about the chance to have input into the decision, the staff met on their own and even drew up blueprints for their proposed design. But when the dust settled, they found themselves working in an expensively remodeled room – built with a straight floor. In the absence of either explanation or action, this chemist switched off. Or as he told research team put together by Daniel Yankelovich: 'My enthusiasm for my company has been beat out of me. So now my enthusiasm is for me. I do a professional job. I can cover my bases. But as far as the fate of my company, as long as there is a signature on my paycheck every week, I couldn't care less – so don't tell me how they are interested in our suggestions for improvements.'

'The reward of a thing well done is to have done it.'
– Ralph Waldo Emerson (1803–1882), American author and philosopher

And finally, consider the experience of an American who worked for a Japanese company that acted promptly on suggestions, but *only* those that led to small cost reductions within each individual department. 'I had a lot of ideas,' she later explained in describing her company's *kaizen taien* (continuous improvement) program, 'but most of them I could never submit because they weren't the kind of ideas our managers wanted to consider. Still we had to submit one idea per year per section member. So we recommended that we only stamp the first page of each fax to head office, rather than every page as required. That fit the rules, and now we only stamp the first page of each fax.'

What kinds of ideas and intelligence does your organization reward? Conversely, which kinds provide negative returns to the information holders – personally costly to provide with few or no likely rewards? And finally, how often do you think your organization passes up intelligence opportunities that are important, if not as world-changing, as the capture of General Lee's 'Lost Order'? Unless your company is highly unusual, there's more for the asking than you might ever dream – but only if you're willing to abide by the arithmetic of the First Law of Intelligent Intelligence Systems.

Part two
The law of diminishing returns:
if and when to act, that is the question

The volume of information that an organization receives is a function of the rewards and punishments given; that's the subject of the First Law. The *value* of that information depends on whether and when this information is used, as laid out in the Second Law of Intelligent Intelligence Systems, which may be stated as follows:

a.   *information is only valuable to the extent to which it is used within the pertinent time frame for action;*

b.   *the pertinent time frame for action is known with precision only after it has expired.*

With this law, we come full cycle back to Boyd's OODA Loop, and two of the risks associated with it. One is acting precipitously; that is, moving to the 'A' stage (action) prematurely, and then carrying out new plans based on highly inadequate or inaccurate information, with predictably poor results. The other is getting stuck on one of the 'O's (observation or orientation) while other players gain relative advantage by moving through the full loop faster and more effectively. When that happens, those who started with superior information or superior position find themselves beaten out of what should have been an easy victory, as General McClellan discovered in the Civil War, General Motors discovered in the Car Wars, and many formerly high-flying companies have discovered in the on-going Microsoft war for total planetary domination.

How do organizations allow themselves to get stuck on one of the 'O's? I think two groups of mechanisms are at play. One has to do with how an enterprise organizes its work in terms of its systems and structures; the other with who it endows with the authority to make the pertinent decisions. Both are discussed briefly in the remainder of this chapter.

'A little neglect may breed mischief ... for want of a nail, the shoe was lost; for want of a shoe, the horse was lost; and for want of a horse, the rider was lost.'
– Benjamin Franklin (1706–1790), American statesman, diplomat, and inventor

Organizational obstacles:
when the wheels of systems and structures grind fine

All organizations have systems and structures – even those that claim to be nonhierarchical and self-organizing do. At minimum there are the informal networks through which items of intelligence pass before action is taken. Then there are the formal policies and procedures that describe which people are supposed to get what information, how they're supposed to proceed, within what timeframes, and the penalties for noncompliance with the official rules. At each step, time is expended and opinions are formed; with each transmittal, details may be embellished or censored, new information may be added or old data deleted. Taken together, all these steps define the organizational OODA Loop for new information, dictating the elapsed time from first intelligence to final action.

'I had suspected for some time now that the Cosmic Command, obviously no longer able to supervise every assignment on an individual basis when there were literally trillions of matters in its charge, had switched over to a random system. The assumption would be that every document, circulating endlessly from desk to desk, must eventually hit upon the right one. A time consuming procedure, perhaps, but one that would never fail.'
– Stanislay Lem, 'Memoirs Found in a Bathtub' (1961)

Some organizations are able to proceed through the loop with reasonable speed relative to the requirements of the situation; others go slower than the competition, with costly consequences. A key discriminator between the two has to do with the kinds of ideas and information that are able to pass through the organizational systems and structures easily and quickly, and the kinds that get stuck on variety of procedural debris.

Sometimes the consequences of such organizational obstacles would be comical if they weren't so sad. Consider the case of an entrepreneurial manager in a leading retail empire who decided to go undercover to observe how customers used his products, and then launched a set of new, redesigned products based on his findings. The good news is that the initiative was quite successful, producing incremental profits of several million dollars for the first year and growing from there. The bad news, however, is that he hadn't hit all the check boxes of the company's TQM program for evaluating new ideas and therefore had to submit the idea and take it through the TQM evaluation as though the new products had never been launched; two years later, the TQM evaluation was still dragging on with no conclusive findings. (Eventually, the process revealed analytically what the test site had shown empirically, and the product was rolled out through the company's entire retail network.)

For the manager in this story, the required retrospective review was more of an annoyance than an obstacle because he had already taken action and the company wasn't about to walk away from the new profit stream he'd created – and because the idea was eventually accepted systemwide. But now consider these questions: how many other ideas, put forth by good corporate citizens who ask before they act, are stuck somewhere in process limbo in your company? And who is reviewing the company's procedures and policies – including, in this case, those related to TQM – to make sure that quest for quality doesn't become a quagmire of check-the-box routines and delay? (Hint: For many organizations, the answers to these two questions are, respectively, 'many', and 'no one'.)

Perhaps most at risk for getting stuck are ideas and initiatives that cross internal organizational boundaries. Please don't tell me that your company has no such internal boundaries because you've gone from 'silos' to 'processes,' or from 'command and control' to 'matrix management.' All you've said in these cases is that you've changed the internal boundaries (and also perhaps how you draw your organization chart), not that you've abolished all boundaries. And therein lies the problem: even in the most open organizations, boundaries between units tend to be semi-permeable at best; that's just a fact of organizational life, romantic theory to the contrary not withstanding. And where boundaries exist, unconventional ideas and unexpected intelligence will get sidetracked, misplaced or vaporized.

Say someone has a great idea or sees a competitive threat, the response to which requires the cooperation of two or more departments. Now say that the departments in question have separate budgets. Who's going to get the increased revenues? Who's going to get dinged for the increased costs? Given bottom-line issues like these, you can be certain that pursuing the idea will require complex intracompany negotiations. From a conceptual point of view, conducting such negotiations in a timely and effective way is important, because such cross-boundary ideas and intelligence-alerts can make enormous differences in future performance, sometimes far bigger than what any one department can do individually. Yet, in practice, the process of coming to agreement can take so long that whatever advantage was gained through early acquisition of critical information and ideas is lost to time spent on internal discussion. When that happens, intelligence that's right on target can still be overwhelmed by organizational obstacles inside the company.

The preference for inaction: extended observation and other grown-up delaying tactics

There's an old joke about the nobleman who committed a petty crime in the presence of the king. The king, as was his custom, gave brief consideration to the data and sentenced the nobleman to be beheaded. 'But sire,' the nobleman protested, 'if you will give me but a year, I will teach this horse to talk.' The king thought it over for a moment and then made his judgment. 'You have a year,' he said. 'If at the end of that year you have gotten this horse to talk, then you shall remain a free man. But if at that time the horse does not talk, then you shall surely die.' After the king made his exit, the nobleman's friend turned to him and whispered, 'What, are you nuts?! You can never get that horse to talk!' To which the aristocrat replied, 'A lot of things can happen in a year. The king could die. I could die … The horse could talk.'

In many organizations, the market may be king, but the executives act like the nobleman in the joke: the more signs pointing to the need for major adjustments in the way they or their companies do business, the more they seek any bargain that will allow them to maintain the status quo. In effect, they create what I think of as 'spacers' in the conversations about what needs to change and the actions that will be required as a result.

How do people create such spacers? Easy. Engage one or multiple consulting firms to review a complex menu of issues, appoint multiple inter-departmental corporate taskforces, or commission a set of major reports, and then stipulate that the work of such groups needs to be completed before new actions are considered. Such spacers are complex and expensive, of course, but more to the point, they're time consuming and they allow the people who would prefer things to stay as they are to put off all new input with a simple, 'That's very interesting, but we need to wait until the ABC report is done or until the XYZ consulting firm had completed its studies.' And then, who knows? The report could come back supporting the status quo; the competitors who have been creating so much trouble could run into their own difficulties; or … the horse could talk.

If you're in situation similar to the one in which the clever nobleman found himself, then you have nothing to lose by such a move; or as my grandfather used to say, 'can't hurt, might help.' But in many business situations, such delays only compound the problem. Then a bad situation continues to deteriorate while opportunities to make the needed improvements are lost to dawdling and procrastination.

In the final analysis, whether the intelligence that comes to and through an organization is acted on in a timely and effective way comes down to the people who have the authority to make the decisions. Intelligence systems provide the input, but the real test is in how and when you use the information once you have it.

'In real life, time is always limited. We can [therefore] never do enough observing or calculating to act with complete confidence.'
– Howard H. Stevenson, author, *Do Lunch or Be Lunch*

• • •

Frequency hopping a signal – or, more generally, spread spectrum signaling – is perhaps the most important concept in modern military communications and radar, and now in commercial wireless communications as well. The basic idea is to vary and spread transmission frequency in order to prevent an adversary from jamming the signal. One of the critical patents on which this field is based was filed in 1941. Its importance is that it provided the first frequency-hopping spread-spectrum technique designed explicitly for the purpose of jamming prevention.

You'd probably guess that the holder of the patent was a well-trained engineer, a ham-radio operator, or a basement inventor. Actually, the patent holder is an unlikely team, Hedy K. Markey and George Antheil. Neither were engineers, nor had studied the prior art in the field. Rather, Antheil was a composer of symphonic music whose closest encounter with the materials in the patent was probably his Ballet Mécanique, which he wrote in the 1920s for a brace of player pianos.

As to Markey, you may not have recognized her by that name. Born Hedwig Eva Maria Kiesler in Austria, she is best known by the stage name that MGM studio honcho, Louis B. Mayer, gave her when she emigrated from Austria in 1938: Hedy Lamarr. Lamarr was one of the most famous and most glamorous movie stars of the 1940s and 50s, and she was convinced that she had an idea that could be critical to US military efforts. Accordingly, when awarded the patent, she and Antheil assigned all rights to the US government. At the time of the patent filing, Lamarr was 27 years old, and perhaps one would have not predicted that her future would include such technical thinking. As M.K. Simon and the co-authors of the text, *Spread Spectrum Communications*, comment, while in Austria, Lamarr had shown 'a flair for innovation' … as evidenced by the fact that age 16, she had '[let] herself be filmed in total nudity while starring in the Czech-produced classic, Ecstasy, the fifth of her many motion pictures.'

A good idea can come from anywhere. So can important information and intriguing impressions. The real question is whether your organization can attract the intelligence it needs – and exploit what it gathers fast enough and effectively enough to make a difference. If not, then all the fancy systems in the world won't allow you to keep pace with an agile competitor that uses the two laws of Intelligent Intelligence Systems to its advantage.

Conclusion

Covert certainties are the devil's playground. They thrive just about anywhere, but especially in those organizations where change is met by patching the overall business system without conscious awareness of the beliefs on which the system is based. Then, as we have seen, even the most pious managers are seduced into committing one or more of the Seven Deadly Sins of Business.

In this respect, the underlying business system of any enterprise can become similar to a legacy computer system. A great example of how such legacy systems take shape and the impacts they can have is provided by a short sidetrip to the year-2000 problem.

One expects a certain amount of silliness with the turn of the millennium. It's the perfect time to announce the emergence of the 'post-modern' era (though I cannot for life of me figure out what 'post modern' could mean), proclaim the ascendance of 'new management paradigms' (regardless of whether the slickly packaged approaches are in fact either new or feasible), and publish stylish books with revolutionary messages that, once parsed, boil down to something along the lines of 'this is the future and you will live in it.' Yet at first glance, the year-2000 problem takes the silliness to previously unimagined heights.

Here's the problem. Computers around the world approached the new century with a two-digit field to indicate year, so that '72' indicated the year 1972 and so on. But this also means that '00' would be interpreted as the year 1900 rather than 2000. Uncorrected, this glitch would create disaster at the turn of the century for any enterprise that worried about schedules, payables and receivables; your business perhaps, and also all the enterprises your business depends on, including banks, airlines, and government agencies.

Solutions exist, but they come with steep price tags. To figure out how steep, use a rough estimate of a buck per line of code, and then consider that a bank like Chase Manhattan has on the order of 200 million lines of code that must be checked. No wonder that J.P. Morgan estimated that fixing the year-2000 problem worldwide would take $200 billion, and that the Gartner Group proposed a worst-case cost of $600 billion. As Holman Jenkins of *The Wall Street Journal* commented, '[even] at the lower figure, the year-2000 problem would still qualify as the most expensive industrial accident of modern times.'

So how did we end up in this mess, given that the two-digit year format was hardly a secret and even school children could have told senior executives that the year after 1999 would be 2000? We got there because when companies first began to convert to large-scale computer systems, memory was exorbitantly expensive, which led to the rational decision to trade future flexibility for current savings. But when it came to pay the piper, the price was complicated by the reality of legacy systems – old computer routines that had been patched and massaged so many times to provide new functions or run on new machines that, after a while, few people knew what had been changed, how it worked, or why. Worse, patches to legacy systems are often done by different people, in computer languages that later become outdated, and without complete and accurate documentation. In consequence, painstaking (and expensive) review of every line of code becomes the only way to fix the resulting problems.

Similarly, the Seven Deadly Sins of Business allow companies to create legacy business systems, ways of doing business that have been patched and massaged so many times that soon few people are focally aware of the changes made or their implications; instead, the adjustments just become part of implicit understanding of what is right and proper in the world and for the enterprise. The question therefore is not whether we are the first generation of managers to experience significant change – we clearly are not – but rather how to make conscious choices about when to keep to the current path and make modest revisions versus when to make substantial alterations, and why.

A summary of sins and the legacy business systems they create

I divided the seven deadly sins of business into three groups; those that affect decisions about strategy (Chapters 1, 2 and 3), organizational design (Chapters 4 and 5), and information flows (Chapters 6 and 7). We can examine how these decisions create counterproductive business systems using the same categories. A look at some final examples tell the tale.

How the Sins of Strategy create patches to the economic model of an enterprise

In 1997, *Harvard Magazine* ran a cover banner on 'Troubled Book Publishing,' which described the strategy patches that have turned the 'marketplace of ideas' into 'just another marketplace' for American consumers. Great editors, such as Maxwell Perkins who collaborated with authors to produce great works, are rare; rather, editors are finding themselves pushed into becoming literary purchasing agents and marketers – even if they have little real marketing experience. And, in business-book publishing, authors are becoming something of an accessory as well, as more and more business books are designed around a proposed selling campaign before pen touches paper (or fingers to keyboard) on the actual content, ghost-written and sometimes also ghost researched, and then sprinkled with essence of author to get a bit of verisimilitude.

Is there a risk in this? Jonathan Galassi, executive editor at Farrar, Straus & Giroux, thinks so. 'Instead of being intrinsic and fundamental, the product becomes incidental to the commercial transaction.' But any commercial transaction, whether for a book or a bagel, depends on providing what customers see as a good deal. This isn't to say I disapprove of book marketing, quite the contrary, I think book marketing is great; bagel marketing too. But that's not the issue for the American book industry. Rather the issue is whether and how long packaging can substitute for, rather than complement, content. I know where I place my bets, which is why I chose two European publishers – Capstone in the UK and Campus in Germany – as the lead publishers for this book. My rationale was simple: in these two companies, editorial and marketing people work as a team, comments to the author are thought provoking and helpful, and – best of all – everyone thinks that reading and understanding the manuscript is a useful thing to do.

Nonetheless, as in all industries, there's almost always more than one economic model that can make sense. Consider Soup Kitchen International, a little take-away shop in Manhattan that sells only soup and bread. Chef–owner Al Yeganeh has a rather unique way of running the operation, which goes like this: decide what soup you want before you get to the counter; have your money ready; place your order and hand over the money; then step *all* the way over to left. Do that, and you'll get your soup and free bread; don't, and you risk being thrown out of the store, or being sent to the back of the line, or getting your soup but not the bread. As Yeganeh puts it: 'Look, you follow my rules? You get free bread. You don't follow my rules? You don't get any … You don't follow the rules and you want bread? Two dollars! The best bread? Five dollars! ... Today, 80 percent of my customers didn't get bread. I felt so bad, but they don't follow my rules!'

Fans of the *Seinfeld* TV sitcom may recognize Yeganeh as similar to a character in one of the show's episodes. Yet despite violation of virtually every tenet of Total Quality Management and Customer Care ideologies, and not withstanding the speedy throughput Yeganeh gets from compliance with his rules, you can still expect a long line at this take-out stand and waiting times of 40 minutes or more. Why? According to the *Zagat* restaurant guide, Yeganeh ladles out some of the best soup on the planet, which is also why his shop received the guide's 'extraordinary to perfection' rating – an honor bestowed on only a handful of Manhattan's, mostly exorbitantly expensive, eateries. As Yeganeh demonstrates, there are lots of way to create a successful economic model, especially if you're aware of the trade-offs inherent in the approach you've chosen to follow.

How the Sins of Organization create patches to the people model of an enterprise

Big steel – the large integrated works that used to dot the American midwest – was once the brightest star in the US economy. But as its luster began to fade in the 1970s and 80s, it went after the enemy it knew – big steel in all the other industrialized and industrializing nations, but most especially Japan. The result was a set of VRAs – 'voluntary' restraint agreements – that limited imports, presumably to give the US industry time to get back on its feet. But the real enemy to the big integrated steel works in the US wasn't the big integrateds abroad, but rather a totally underestimated enemy at home – the US minimills.

Minimills use different inputs and equipment than the integrateds do – scrap steel and electric arc furnaces for the minimills; iron ore, sinter mills, coke batteries, blast furnaces and basic oxygen furnaces for the big guys. So what kept the integrateds from closing down their outdated mills and moving to more minimill-like configurations for selected products? There were the usual sins of both strategy and information, but one of the biggest barriers was the legacy people model.

Here's what happened. In 1974, the industry put into place a novel kind of labor contract, known as the ENA, or experimental negotiating agreement. The deal was that the companies secured a no-strike agreement, and in exchange, the workers received substantial wage increases and income protections. The belief was that the ENA would be an import fighter, by ensuring that foreign steel wouldn't penetrate the US market during any future strike. In fact, the last industry-wide strike had been fifteen years before, in 1959. And worse, once in place, the ENA backfired by making shut-downs of outdated facilities hideously expensive. As one example, when Bethlehem Steel finally shut down its Lackawanna Works in New York in the mid 1980s, the required payments to the workers forced the company to take close to a billion dollar write-off. In addition, the agreement made it all but impossible for the integrateds to follow the lead of minimills, such as Nucor, that used aggressive gain-sharing programs to keep both workers and management striving for the same goals. The ENA, meant to give flexibility, instead became an organizational manacle.

But, as with strategic models, one organizational approach does not fit all. Consider Mondragón, a multi-national conglomerate headquartered in the Basque region of Spain. The enterprise is often touted as the model for the new-age organization due to its industrial worker ownership, its relatively egalitarian compensation system (the difference between the highest paid and the lowest is six times, versus a hundred times or more in the US), its cooperative governance structure (the Mondragón Corporación Coopertiva), and its reinvestment of surpluses into both new ventures and into an education and promotion fund for its members.

Can this system be duplicated elsewhere? The people of Mondragón aren't sure that it can. Or, as one confided to *Financial Times* reporter David White, 'We are not even sure if it would have worked if it had started in Spain today rather than back in the 1950s.' Organizations are delicate things. It helps if you think about what you are doing, why, and possible consequences, rather than blindly follow what some other enterprise has done.

How the Sins of Information
create patches to the knowledge model of an enterprise

Read the headlines in any given year in any given country, and you'll find a whole slew of sorry executives who were surprised by some unfortunate event that had negative effects on their business (or positive ones for a competitor). Scratch the surface, and you'll usually find that the warning signs were present somewhere in the organization, but either didn't make it to the people who needed to see them, or were transmitted but ignored until too late.

Prudential Insurance Co. of America, which in 1996 agreed to a settlement of at least $410 million to resolve a class-action suit concerning deceptive sales practices, provides a classic example. As *The Wall Street Journal* later reported, 'At the time [1996], state regulators said that top Prudential officials should have known of widespread problems as early as 1992. But hundreds of pages of internal documents reviewed by *The Wall Street Journal* ... show that board members and top executives were told of such practices a decade earlier [1982], and that they were warned in several successive years that the problems hadn't been resolved.' Fourteen years from first warning to final judgment is a pretty good lead time, but it's as useless as no data at all if the warnings aren't heeded.

Or consider the 1997 death of a freshman at the Massachusetts Institute of Technology who died of acute alcohol poisoning after drinking heavily at an MIT fraternity party. *The Boston Globe* subsequently reported that a committee of students, faculty and administrators had submitted a report on the problem six years before, in 1991, including the statistic that something on the order of ten to twenty percent of fraternity members admitted to consuming, on occasion, five or more drinks per sitting. A year later, two students, Scott R. Velazquez and Robert Plotnick, wrote a letter to MIT president Charles Vest and, after receiving little response of substance, sent a second letter in 1993 which said, in part, 'When a student is killed or dies at an MIT fraternity, how will MIT explain its full knowledge of dangerous and illegal practices persisting unchecked over a period of years?' It's an eerie quote to read after the fact, and terribly sad as well.

Though not as dramatic, customers, employees and suppliers routinely see early signs of opportunities and threats but then can't get the right people to listen, can't get them to act, or have decided that it's not even worth their while to try to do either. Who's responsible here? In all cases, primary responsibility starts at the top. Show me a dysfunctional approach to seeing and transmitting information, and I'll show you a management team that encourages misuse of data. (Of course, the data don't go away in this scenario; they just become more useful to some other enterprise than to yours.)

Of managers and leaders …
… and moving from OODA Loops to BOODA Loops

In Tudor times, if I understand my English history correctly, it was common practice to camp in one castle, befoul it, and then when the filth and stench became unbearable, to move to the next so the first could be cleaned and aired. I sometimes think we have done the same with the language of business. Now, dissatisfied with the decisions that managers make, we decide that the problem is with management itself; that we need to move to a new, good concept – leadership – and thereby leave the old, bad concept – management – someplace in the dust. Just like the court population, we pollute the old word and then move to a new one with high hopes of a different outcome.

But changing the words doesn't change the reality (though it does sell books). The problem is not one of too many managers and too few leaders. Rather the problem starts with poor managerial decisions that lead an organization into one or more the Seven Deadly Sins of Business. And this in turn brings me back to Boyd's OODA Loop, which has been a theme through this book. But now I want to make a revision, by placing one step before the first 'O.' In my conception, the required insert is 'B' for 'beliefs.' The reason for this change is simple. Moving faster through the OODA Loop will not help you if the beliefs on which you based your business system are flawed; in that case, you'll continue to do the wrong things, but now faster and more efficiently than ever before and, if you're really unlucky, faster and more efficiently than your competitors.

The revised BOODA Loop looks like this:

- *Beliefs:* make beliefs explicit so you can reduce risk of being blindsided by covert certainties;

- *Observation:* search actively to see what's happening around you, as well as to understand the consequences of previous actions;

- *Orientation:* place yourself within the evolving situation and associated time constraints, and generate options (including doing nothing);

- *Decision:* mentally 'run the camera forward' on each of the options to forecast likely results and then select one; and

- *Action:* take the selected action in timely fashion, observe the actual consequences and use the new data to challenge your implicit beliefs.

Now with the initial 'B' in place, you can engage in real learning; not the antiseptic learning of reviewing flow diagrams and consultants' reports, but the messy, disruptive, effective learning that takes place when you have the courage to challenge your own beliefs and are willing to endure the pain that comes with giving up the security provided by unquestioned assumptions. And with that comes one of the real differentiators between poor managers and good ones: the willingness and ability to 'see around the corners' and then take action – the prerequisite for deciding when to make modest changes and when to make radical ones.

Are you willing to commit to the BOODA Loop? If so, and in the spirit of this book, I'd like to offer my Ten Commandments for Freeing the Corporate Mind for your consideration. Follow these, and your risk of managing with the best of intentions and still ending up in a doom-loop will abate appreciably:

- Management is first and foremost about thinking, and then taking action. Working in an environment of change and incomplete data is not a mitigating factor. All managers work in environments of change and incomplete data to greater or lesser extents. And that's in fact what managers get paid for, to make difficult decisions with incomplete information in environments of continuous and shifting change.

- All business systems change over time. If you want to keep your business system from slipping into a destructive legacy loop, start by challenging your own beliefs in three key areas: (1) how the world really works; (2) what your organization needs to do in terms of its strategy, organization design, and information flows, to operate within this evolving environment; and (3) why the people who are part of the organization will be better off if they make the adjustments than if they stick with the status quo as the environment shifts.

- Your real strategy is what you do, not what you say you do. Look first at your budget numbers and investment requisitions, rather than at your plans, to figure out what your company's real strategy is. (This also works for one's own life strategy as well.)

- The product, and the benefits it provides, is the core of all strategy. But product concepts are defined in use, not in conference rooms. If you want to understand how the market will evolve and what changes you could or will need to make, start by looking at what people actually do or could want to do with the products in question and why, rather than what you think they should do.

- Whatever the mission of your enterprise, you have to meet the 'good deal at a profit over time' standard. But the game you have to play to meet this standard is always mutating. If you don't keep checking to see if your understanding of the real rules of this mutating game is keeping up with the changes, chances are it isn't.

- The strategy of an enterprise is not a thing apart from its people. Rather, the people of an enterprise enact the strategy daily, a hundred or so times per person. But the only way these tiny – and not so tiny – actions add up on the plus side of the ledger is if two requirements are met: the people possess the judgment and ability to do more than the minimum, and they possess the willingness to do so. Slogans are nice, but investments – of time and money, heart and attention – are essential.

- Treating people like widgets is a good way to increase the odds that your company will be one in which the workforce has become a formidable handicap rather than an asset, even if the level of innate ability is high. The only solution: adhere to the 'fair deal at a profit over time' standard and keep checking to assess whether the current deal provide both sides with adequate levels of the WIF-MEs each seeks.

- All of us see the world through the double lenses of our expectations and preferences. Real learning starts when beliefs change. And changing beliefs requires the personal discipline to see what we don't expect and prefer to see, which in turn frequently involves a fair bit of discomfort or even pain. Or as President Harry Truman, known as 'Give-'em Hell' Harry, once said: 'I never did give anybody hell. I just told them the truth and they thought it was hell.'

- Most of what you need to know is already resident somewhere within your organization; the question is whether you are willing to remove the obstacles that keep important intelligence from reaching the right people in a timely fashion, or keep the people from making the right decisions in a timely fashion.

- No matter where you sit in your organization, the buck stops with you.

Beliefs impel to action. Whether you help take your organization heavenward or elsewhere is up to you. The path isn't always easy, but oh – think of the alternative.

Last Word

*If I see that a company
is substituting money for thinking,
I short the stock.*

– Peter Drucker

Acknowledgments

Fate plays strange tricks. In the case of this book, the tricks in question had to do with two of the foreign rights publishers for *Fad Surfing in the Boardroom* – Capstone Publishing Limited in the UK and Campus Verlag in Germany – and the publicity tours each invited me to do in their respective countries. After I had met the key people in each company, I made a firm decision on my final evening in London. I would do another book, but only if I could convince Capstone and Campus to be the publishers. My reasoning was simple. The people were great, and the company strategies made sense – an absolute revelation for an American author.

So the first thanks for this book go to the people in those two companies. Mark Allin, Richard Burton and Catherine Meyrick are the principals at Capstone. It would be difficult to thank them sufficiently. The heart of the publishing world in the US is in my backyard: Boston and New York. Capstone sits in Oxford, thousands of miles and five time zones away. Yet the collaboration I've had with Capstone has gone beyond my expectations in every area: what I had to say, how I should say it, and how we would market the resulting book. There's a bit of irony in this; when I originally looked into whether we could sell the UK rights for *Fad Surfing*, I was told to forget it as the book market in the UK was a disaster, and that all the UK publishers were too. What do you know? Even New Yorkers can hold beliefs that are worth challenging.

Campus Verlag, the German language publisher for *The Seven Deadly Sins of Business*, was founded by Frank Schwoerer, and the team there has grown to include his son, Thomas C. Schwoerer, Bettina Querfurth, Regina Eisele, and a whole crew of other professionals. As with the folks at Capstone, the people at Campus are exceptional. I feel particularly lucky that I was able to meet and spend time with Frank before he died in 1997. The literature I've read on German business argues that successful entrepreneurs in that country start their businesses when they are young, say in their twenties. Fortunately, Frank didn't read these books. Born in 1925, he founded Campus when he was in his late forties, because, as he told me, he had been fired from his job at an American publisher and needed to do something to support himself and his family. The result is a great company, a wonderful legacy of a wonderful man.

My thanks are also due to Tom Fryer, a principal of Sparks Computer Solutions in Oxford, who typeset this book, and put up with a variety of obsessions, peccadilloes and outrageous demands on the part of the author, who would, of course, be me. I was constantly impressed by the professionalism and speed of both Tom and Sparks, and think this book looks terrific due to his efforts. As to the speed, the process that Tom used was an order of magnitude – literally ten times – faster than what I have seen at US publishers. It's a pleasure to work with a publisher and a designer who think that time is not just a variable to write about, but also is a component of a book-publishing strategy.

I am also grateful to Steven J. Bennett who, as usual, acted as my master drill sergeant on every draft of this book. Steve is unflinchingly honest, an irritating habit, but one that is essential for real learning. Usually what I learned with Steve was that what I had done wasn't good enough and I needed to go back to the drawing board, which I did innumerable times until Steve told me that I had something that might be okay. I took most but not all of Steve recommendations. You can therefore be sure that those places where the logic isn't as tight as it should be or where the text reads funny is where I neglected to follow his advice.

The content of this book was significantly enriched by several people. Tom Brown, of Management General, kicked me until I wrote the way I talk instead of the way somebody taught to me write when I was in school. He also suggested the theme of the Seven Deadly Sins, and was indefatigable in giving feedback and suggestions, even when he disagreed with my line of reasoning. You can get a taste of Tom's exploration of management issues by visiting his innovative web site at <http://www. mgeneral.com>. Another Tom, Tom Cummings, of Leading Ventures BV and who I met courtesy of Felix Twaalfhoven, has added a number of fascinating insights and introduced me to a number of fascinating people who pushed me to think in fresh ways about complicated topics. Among these many people is Ian McMonagle, who brings a wonderful perspective to the human side of business.

Mike Chisek, of DC Capital, did a fine-tooth-comb read of several of the chapters, and helped me push my thinking forward. Since Mike is always right and never lies, I know I was in good hands. Bruce Sunstein did all the legal work, and as usual provided great intellectual counsel as well as legal counsel. Barbara Rosenkrantz, Professor of the History of Science at Harvard University, helped me get my facts right in the discussion about change and the role of the manager. Robert Eccles and Nitin Nohria, whose name I can now spell correctly, were both invaluable in thinking through how to conduct the research at the Beth Israel Hospital. And thanks to Robin Brown, General Manager of the Boston Four Seasons, for providing great answers to crazy questions about a busboy, despite still being jet lagged from a business trip to Saudi Arabia from which he had just returned.

The Rabkins have also contributed substantially to this book. Adrienne Rabkin put me onto the hunt to learn more about John Boyd and his OODA Loop. Thanks also to Mitchell Rabkin MD, CEO of what is now known as the Care Group – a health care systems composed of the Beth Israel Hospital, New England Deaconess Hospital, Mount Auburn Hospital among others – who opened the BI to Elizabeth Glaser and me with absolutely no restrictions on the research described in Chapter 5.

Three journalists may see their footprints in this book. Johanna Zugmann of *Der Standard* in Vienna, pushed me to think about the nature of change. She interviewed me during a boat ride down the Danube and asked me questions about change that got me to thinking about the Viennese manager I described in the Introduction. And it was a question from Heiko Ernst, editor of *Psychologie Heute*, about my 'meta-philosophy' that led to the Ten Commandments for Freeing The Corporate Mind, which are presented in the Conclusion. T George Harris, former editor of *American Psychology Today* and *Harvard Business Review*, not only introduced me to Heiko, but helped me to think through what 'covert certainties' are and how they drive behavior.

My old finance teacher, Eric Rosenfeld, will finally know that I did pay attention when he taught us about not running out of cash, the mechanics of finance, and the lure of 32 Red. I wish I had paid closer attention; Eric is now rightly considered one of the preeminent geniuses in the investment world and has the track record to prove the claim.

And then there the many people who, over the years debated the ideas or contributed the stories that have gone into this book. These include: Kathleen Alexander, Ed Baron, Robert Bettacchi, Amar Bhide, Jeff Bradach, Robert Buzzell, Carol Franco, Robert Keefe, Tony Lloyd, John Mahaney, Rand Mulford, Bob Nelson, Susan Plimpton, Jim Ramsey, Jeremy Silverman, Trina Soske, Beth Stern, Mary Sutherland, Marjorie Williams, Susan Webber, Susan Weiler, as well as the many clients with whom I have been privileged to work and from whom I have learned. And, of course, thanks to Ben. What would a book of sins be without him?

Bibliography

Many of the examples in this book and accompanying background data come from personal observation, were related to me during interviews I conducted, or were shared over the course of conversations. I've also built on the thinking of an older book that I wrote some years ago, *How Corporate Truths Become Competitive Traps* (New York: John Wiley & Sons, 1991, now out of print), and I've used a few of the examples from that text in this book as well. In the interest of saving trees, for the most part, I have not included articles for major news stories that are well known, such as the Barings case, in this bibliography. The rest of the bibliography follows.

Introduction

Barker, Joel Arthur. *Paradigms: The Business of Discovering the Future*. New York: HarperBusiness, 1992.

Christie, Agatha. *The Murder of Roger Ackroyd*. New York: Dodd, Mead & Company, 1926.

de Geus, Arie. 'Planning as Learning.' *Harvard Business Review*, March–April 1988, pp. 70–74.

Edmunds, Marlene. 'Philips quitting media biz, exept for Polygram stake.' *Daily Variety*, 22 July 1997, p. 4.

Forman, Craig . 'Lloyd's of London, an insurance bulwark, is a firm under siege.' *The Wall Street Journal*, 24 October 1989, pp. A1, A20.

Halberstam, David. *The Reckoning*. New York: Avon Books, 1986.

Ingrassia, Lawrence and Milbank, Dana. 'Hit by huge losses, Lloyd's of London struggles to survive.' *The Wall Street Journal*, 15 May 1995, pp. A1, A6.

Janis, Irving L. 'Groupthink,' in Andrew D. Szilangyi and Marc J. Wallace Jr, eds, *Readings in Organizational Behavior and Performance*. Santa Monica, CA: Goodyear Publishing Co., 1980.

Kuhn, Thomas. *The Structure of Scientific Revolutions* (2nd edn, enlarged). Chicago, IL: University of Chicago Press, 1970.

Lohr, Steve. 'The future came faster in the old days.' *The New York Times*, 5 October 1997, Section 4, pp. 1, 4.

Rebello, Kathy. 'Inside Microsoft.' *BusinessWeek*, 15 July 1996, pp. 56 ff.

Shapiro, Eileen C. 'Managing in the Age of Gurus.' *Harvard Business Review*, March–April 1997, pp. 142 ff.

Shapiro, Eileen C. *Fad Surfing in the Boardroom*. Reading, MA: Addison-Wesley, 1995; Oxford: Capstone Publishing Ltd, 1996.

Stevenson, Howard H. *Do Lunch or Be Lunch*. Boston, MA: Harvard Business School Press, 1998.

'Time line: a rich century of better mousetraps.' *Newsweek Special Issue: The Power of Invention*, Winter 1997–98, pp. 12–15.

'The evolution of the calculator.' *The New York Times*, 1 September 1997, p. D3.

'Lloyd's of London: solvent abuse.' *The Economist*, 29 April 1995, p. 88.

Quotes and sidebars throughout

Andrew, Robert. *The Concise Columbia Dictionary of Quotations*. New York: Avon Books, 1987.

Byrne, Robert. *1,911 Best Things Anybody Ever Said*. New York: Ballantine Books, 1988.

Crainer, Stuart. *The Ultimate Book of Business Quotations*. Oxford: Capstone Publishing Ltd, 1997.

Platt, Suzy, ed. *Respectfully Quoted: A Dictionary from the Library of Congress*. Washington, DC: Congressional Quarterly, Inc., 1992.

Sources used throughout

Boyd, John R. *A Discourse on Winning and Losing*. Air University Library, Maxwell Air Force Base, Report No. MU 43947, August 1987.

Hirschman, Albert O. *Exit, Voice, and Loyalty*. Cambridge, MA: Harvard University Press, 1970.

Kuhn, Thomas. *The Structure of Scientific Revolutions* (2nd edn, enlarged). Chicago, IL: University of Chicago Press, 1970.

Shapiro, Eileen C. *Fad Surfing in the Boardroom*. Reading, MA: Addison-Wesley, 1995; Oxford: Capstone Publishing Ltd, 1996.

Stevenson, Howard H. *Do Lunch or Be Lunch*. Boston, MA: Harvard Business School Press, 1998.

Sin #1

Adcarelli, Silvia. 'Dell finds U.S. strategy works in Europe.' *The Wall Street Journal*, 3 February 1997, p. A8.

Bennett, Steven J. and Snell, Michael. *Executive Chess*. New York: New American Library, 1987.

Bick, Julie. *All I Really Need to Know in Business I Learned at Microsoft*. New York: Pocket Books, 1997.

Byrne, John A. 'Strategic planning: it's back!' *BusinessWeek*, 26 August 1996, pp. 46–52.

Carton, Barbara. 'Swimsuits grow up with the boomers.' *The Boston Globe*, 30 May 1989, p. 31.

Clayman, Michelle. 'In search of excellence: the investor's viewpoint,' *Financial Analysts' Journal*, May–June 1987, pp. 54–63.

Garry, Greg. 'Maxtor's plan.' *Electronic Buyers' News*, 9 July 1990, p. 3.

Hansell, Saul. 'A scoundrel or a scapegoat? A ruling will soon set Joseph Jett's place in Wall St. lore.' *The New York Times*, 6 April 1997, Section 3, pp. 1, 8.

Keller, Maryann. *Rude Awakening*. New York: William Morrow and Company, Inc., 1989.

Kupfer, Andrew. 'America's fastest-growing company.' *Fortune*, 13 August 1990, pp. 48 ff.

Lagnado, Lucette. 'Ex-manager describes the profit-driven life inside Columbia/HCA.' *The Wall Street Journal*, 30 May 1997, pp. A1, A6.

Lele, Milind. *The Customer is Key*. New York: John Wiley & Sons, 1987.

Narisetti, Raju. 'Move to drop coupons puts Procter & Gamble in sticky PR situation.' *The Wall Street Journal*, 17 April 1997, pp. A1, A10.

Peters, Thomas J. and Waterman, Robert H. Jr. *In Search of Excellence*. New York: Harper & Row, 1982.

Porter, Michael. *Competitive Strategy*. New York: The Free Press, 1980.

Reis, Al and Trout, Jack. *Marketing Warfare*. New York: New American Library, 1986.

Ricks, David A. *Big Business Blunders*. Homewood, IL: Dow Jones-Irwin, 1983.

Rebello, Kathy. 'Inside Microsoft: The untold story of how the Internet forced Bill Gates to reverse his corporate strategy.' *BusinessWeek*, 15 July 1996, pp. 56–67.

Robichaux, Mark. 'Tabasco-sauce maker remains hot after 125 years.' *The Wall Street Journal*, 11 May 1990, p.B2.

Russo, J. Edward and Schoemaker, Paul J.H. *Decision Traps*. New York: Doubleday/Currency, 1989.

Sculley, John. *Odyssey*. New York: Harper & Row, 1987.

Sowell, Thomas. 'Turning 60, looking back.' *The Boston Herald*, 7 July 1990, p. 15.

Stecklow, Steve. 'Kentucky's teachers get bonuses, but some are caught cheating.' *The Wall Street Journal*, 2 September 1997, pp. A1, A5.

Trachtenberg, Jeffrey A. 'How Philips flubbed its U.S. introduction of electronic product.' *The Wall Street Journal*, 28 June 1996, pp. A1, A4.

Zemke, Ron. *The Service Edge*. New York: New American Library, 1989.

Zipper, Stuart. 'MiniScribe: criminal indictments expected.' *Electronic News*, 19 August 1991, p. 1.

Zipper, Stuart. 'Maxtor buying MiniScribe.' *Electronic News*, 9 April 1990, p. 1.

Zipser, Andy. 'Cooking the books: how pressure to raise sales led MiniScribe to falsify numbers.' *The Wall Street Journal*, 11 September 1989, pp. A 1, A8.

Zipser, Andy. 'MiniScribe's investigators determine that "massive fraud" was perpetrated.' *The Wall Street Journal*, 12 September 1989, p. A6.

'MiniScribe CEO guilty, could get 15 years in jail.' *Newsbytes News Network*, 29 August 1994.

'MiniScribe investors awarded $550 million.' *Electronic News*, 10 February 1992, p. 9.

'Komatsu: Ryoichi Kawai's Leadership.' Harvard Business School Case 9-390-037. Boston, MA: The President and Fellows of Harvard College, 1989.

'Caterpillar Tractor Company.' Harvard Business School Case 9-385-276. Boston, MA: The President and Fellows of Harvard College, 1985.

'Komatsu Limited.' Harvard Business School Case 9-385-277. Boston, MA: The President and Fellows of Harvard College, 1985.

'Note on the Watch Industries in Switzerland, Japan and the

United States – 1950-70.' Harvard Business School Case 9-373-090. Boston, MA: The President and Fellows of Harvard College, 1973.

'Timex Corp.' Harvard Business School Case 9-373-080. Boston, MA: The President and Fellows of Harvard College, 1973.

Sin #2:

Bennett, Amanda and Hymowitz, Carol. 'For customers, more than lip service?' *The Wall Street Journal*, 6 October 1989, p. Bl.

Bick, Julie. *All I Really Need to Know in Business I Learned at Microsoft*. New York: Pocket Books, 1997.

Boyd, John R. *A Discourse on Winning and Losing*. Air University Library, Maxwell Air Force Base, Report No. MU 43947, August 1987.

Bradburn, Elizabeth and Miller, Annetta. 'Take a hike, cruel shoes.' *Newsweek*, 14 May 1990, p. 48.

Burns, James MacGregor. *Leadership*. New York: Harper Torchbooks, 1978.

Carton, Barbara. 'Swimsuits grow up with the boomers.' *The Boston Globe*, 30 May 1989, p. 31.

Chase, Marilyn. 'Health Journal: New fall fashions put the ouch back into women's shoes.' *The Wall Street Journal*, 13 October 1997, p. B1.

Elsner, David M. 'Microwave ovens prove hot sellers despite recession.' *The Wall Street Journal*, 22 April 1979, p. 31.

Hirsch, James S. 'Questions about U.S. Shoe Corp. continue to mount.' *The Wall Street Journal*, 5 April 1990, p. A6.

Hof, Robert D. 'Where did the Net come from, Daddy?' *BusinessWeek*, 16 September 1996, p. 19; review of Hafner, Katie and Lyon, Matthew. *Where Wizards Stay Up Late: The Origins of the Internet*. New York: Simon & Schuster, 1996.

Jefferson, David J. 'Litton Industries' microwave-oven business is sold.' *The Wall Street Journal*, 22 August 1988.

Magaziner, Ira C. and Patinkin, Mark. 'Fast heat: how Korea won the microwave war.' *The Harvard Business Review*, January–February 1989, pp. 83–92.

McCarthy, Michael J. 'Food companies hunt for a "next big thing" but few can find one.' *The Wall Street Journal*, 6 May 1997, pp. A1, A8.

Nash, Bruce and Zullo, Allan. *The MisFortune 500*. New York: Pocket Books, 1988.

Newman, Barry. 'Dutch are invading JFK arrivals building and none too soon.' *The Wall Street Journal*, 13 May 1997, pp. A1, A8.

Rebello, Kathy. 'Inside Microsoft: the untold story of how the Internet forced Bill Gates to reverse his corporate strategy.' *BusinessWeek*, 15 July 1996, pp. 56–67.

Ryan, Suzanne C. 'Tonight's homework: try on a bikini.' *The Boston Globe*, 19 March 1997, pp. D1, D6.

Shanklin, William L. *Six Timeless Marketing Blunders*. Lexington, MA: Lexington Books, 1989.

Siwolop, Sana. 'Orphans of invention: great minds, small money.' *The New York Times*, 9 March 1997, p. 16.

Slywotzky, Adrian J. *Value Migration*. Boston, MA: Harvard Business School Press, 1996.

Thurow, Roger. 'In global drive, Nike finds its brash ways don't always pay off.' *The Wall Street Journal*, 5 May 1997.

White, Diane. 'Stilettos get a toehold on fashion.' *The Boston Globe*, 14 October 1997, p. C6.

'Cooking equipment.' *Market Share Reporter*, 1998, pp. 853, 855.

'Microwave ovens.' *Consumer Reports*, November 1986.

HFD, 11 May 1985.

'Amana Microwave Ovens.' Harvard Business School Case 9-579-182, revised. Boston, MA: The President and Fellows of Harvard College, 1984.

'General Electric Microwave Ovens.' Harvard Business School Case 9-579-184, revised. Boston, MA: The President and Fellows of Harvard College, 1984.

Merchandising Week, September 1983.

Merchandising Week, March 1983.

'Can Japanese makers take the heat?' *HFD*, 29 March 1982, p. 32.

'Confident execs plan for market domination.' *HFD*, 18 December 1978, p. 134.

'Litton Microwave Cooking Products (C).' Harvard Business School Case 9-477-085. Boston, MA: The President and Fellows of Harvard College, 1977.

'Note on the Microwave Oven Industry.' Harvard Business School Case 9-579-185. Boston, MA: The President and Fellows of Harvard College, 1979.

Sin #3

Bronson, Gail. 'Watching the wrong birdie.' *Forbes*, 28 April 1986, pp. 96, 100.

Chapman, Mark. 'Hotel has reservations about room for three.' *The Boston Herald*, 25 May 1997, pp. 71–2.

D'Aveni, Richard A. *Hypercompetition*. New York: The Free Press, 1994.

Fabricant, Florence. 'Champions of breakfast.' *The New York Times*, 17 May 1997, pp. 23, 25.

Gates, Bill and Ballmer, Steve. 'Focus on technology: how we did it.' *Newsweek*, 23 June 1997, pp. 78 ff.

Gibson, Richard. 'Broad grocery price cuts may not pay.' *The Wall Street Journal*, 7 May 1993, p. B1.

Grossfield, Stan. 'Polaroid takes another shot at instant success.' *The Boston Globe*, 3 April 1986, pp. 61 ff.

Hammonds, Keith H. 'Polaroid's Spectra may be losing its flash,' *Business Week*, 29 June 1987, pp. 31–2.

Hoch, Stephen J., Dreze, Xavier, and Purk, Mary E. 'EDLP [every day low pricing], hi-lo, and margin arithmetic.' Graduate School of Business, University of Chicago, August 1993.

Kleinfield, N.R. 'How Cuisinart lost its edge.' *The New York Times*

Magazine, 15 April 1990, pp. 46 ff.

Kristof, Nicolas D. 'Polaroid bets on new camera; more affluent buyer sought.' *The New York Times*, 3 April 1986, p. D1.

Micklethwait, John and Wooldridge, Adrian. *The Witch Doctors*. New York: Times Books, 1996.

Schnaars, Steven P. *Megamistakes*. New York: The Free Press, 1989.

Shapiro, Eban. 'New price move by Philip Morris intensifies war.' *The Wall Street Journal*, 21 July 1993, pp. B1, B8.

Shapiro, Eban. 'Price cut on Marlboro upsets rosey notions about tobacco profits. *The Wall Street Journal*, 5 April 1993, pp. A1, A10.

Wensberg, Peter C. *Land's Polaroid*. Boston, MA: Houghton Mifflin, 1987.

Los Angeles Times. 'Ratings plummet for TV, printed news.' *The Boston Globe*, 21 March 1997, p. A13.

'Kellogg slashes prices; Ralcorp schedules downsizing.' *Milling and Baking News*, 18 June 1996.

'Cereal pricing moves have broad implications.' *Milling and Baking News*, 18 June 1996.

'Post reduces cereal prices, changes couponing strategy.' *Supermarket News*, 22 April 1996.

'Elastic brands.' *The Economist*, 19 November 1994, p. 75.

'Philip Morris: Man Friday.' *The Economist*, 25 June 1994, p. 65.

'When smoke got in their eyes.' *The Economist*, 10 April 1993, pp. 65–6.

'The search for El Dorado.' *The Economist*, 16 May 1992, pp. 21–4.

Sin #4

Beatty, Sally Goll. 'Marlboro's billboard man may soon ride into the sunset.' *The Wall Street Journal*, 1 July 1997, pp. B1, B8.

Beckham, J. Daniel. 'Winners: strategies of ten of America's most successful hospitals.' *Health Forum Journal*, November/December 1989, pp. 17–23.

Boyd, John R. *A Discourse on Winning and Losing.* Air University Library, Maxwell Air Force Base, Report No. MU 43947, August 1987.

Byrne, John A. 'Profiting from the nonprofits: much can be learned from some of the best-run organizations around.' *BusinessWeek*, 26 March 1990, pp. 66 ff.

Carlzon, Jan. *Moments of Truth.* Cambridge, MA: Ballinger Publishing Company, 1987.

Cohen, Allan R. and Bradford, David L. *Influence Without Authority.* New York: John Wiley & Sons, 1990.

Evans, John S. *The Management of Human Capacity.* Bradford, West Yorkshire: MCB Publications, 1978.

Guest. 'Of time and the foreman.' *Personnel*, Vol. 32, 1956, pp. 478–86.

Jacobs, Sally. 'Hold the hostility.' *The Boston Globe*, 25 February 1993, p. G1.

Jaques, Elliott. *A General Theory of Bureaucracy.* London: Heinemann, 1976.

Jaques, Elliott. *Requisite Organization.* Arlington, VA: Cason Hall, 1989.

Mintzberg, Henry. *The Nature of Managerial Work.* New York: Harper & Row, 1973.

Sunshine, Linda and Wright, John W. *The Best Hospitals in America.* New York: Henry Holt and Company, 1987.

Zemke, Ron. *The Service Edge: 101 Companies that Profit from Customer Care.* New York: New American Library, New York, 1989.

Sin #5

Adams, Jane Meredith. 'Wearing the union label in Calif.' *The Boston Globe*, 2 September 1996, p. A5.

Adelson, Andrea. 'Physician, unionize thyself.' *The New York Times*, 5 April 1997, pp. 27–8.

Aeppel, Timothy. 'Not all workers find idea of empowerment as neat as it sounds.' *The Wall Street Journal*, 8 November 1997, pp. A1, A10.

Allen, Henry. 'Thanks, folks. See ya. In the cash-driven '90s, loyalty will get you a pat on the head. And a kick in the rear.' *The Washington Post*, 15 February 1996, p. C1, C8.

Brown, DeNeen L. 'Cosby warns GWU grads: it gets harder by degrees.' *The Washington Post*, 19 May 1997, pp. B1, B7.

Burkins, Glenn. 'Temp workers may be able to join unions.' *The Wall Street Journal*, 2 December 1996, p.A3.

Eliot, George. *Felix Holt*, first published in 1866; New York: Everyman Library Edition, 1997.

Exotic Dancers Union. http://www.baysan.org/EDAunion.

Fritsch, Peter; Sullivan, Allanna; and Sharpe, Rochelle. 'Texaco to pay $176.1 million in bias suit.' *The Wall Street Journal*, 18 November 1996, pp. A3, A6.

Hammer, Michael and Champy, James. *Reengineering the Corporation: A Manifesto for Business Revolution*. New York: HarperBusiness, 1993.

Lewis, Diane E. 'Hoteling lets "concierges" book worker office space.' *The Boston Globe*, 7 November 1995, p. 44.

Lewis, Diane E. 'Temporary workers seek equal status to join unions.' *The Boston Globe*, 4 March 1997.

Nash, Bruce and Zullo, Allan. *The MisFortune 500*. New York: Pocket Books, 1988.

Rodger, Will. 'Corporate threat: attack of the slamming sites.' *Inter@ctive Week*, 22 July 1996, pp. 18–22.

Schwartz, Peter, and Kelly, Kevin. 'The relentless contrarian.' *Wired*, August 1996, pp. 116 ff.

Shapiro, Eileen C. 'The "Glow and Tingle" Audit.' *The Wall Street Journal*, 26 February 1996.

Tilly, Chris and Uchitelle, Louis. 'More downsized workers are returning as rentals.' *The New York Times*, 8 December 1996, pp. 1, 34.

Verespej, Michael. 'More employment mandates? An aggressive NRLB and unsettled employment issues have business worried.' *IndustryWeek*, 3 February 1997, pp. 24–6.

Wells, Susan J. 'For stay-home workers, speed bumps on the telecommute.' *The New York Times*, 17 August 1997, Section 3, p. 1.

White, Joseph B. 'Re-engineering gurus take steps to remodel their stalling vehicles.' *The Wall Street Journal*, 26 November 1996, pp. A1, A13.

Yankelovich, Daniel; Zetterberg, Hans; Strumpel, Burkhard; Shanks, Michael; Immerwahr, John; Noelle-Neumann, Elisabeth; Sengoku, Tamotsu; and Yuchtman-Yaar, Ephraim. *The World at Work: An International Report on Jobs, Productivity, and Human Values*. New York: Octagon Books, 1985.

Zemke, Ron. 'In defense of fad surfing.' *Training*, September 1995, p. 8.

'Girl Scout cookie protest leader removed from her position.' The Associated Press, 3 July 1997.

'Girl Scout troops insist on more cookie profits.' *Louisville Courier-Journal*, 22 January 1997.

'Texaco execs discuss lawsuit.' *Los Angeles Sentinel*, 7 November 1996, p. A13.

Sin #6

Boyd, John R. *A Discourse on Winning and Losing*. Air University Library, Maxwell Air Force Base, Report no. MU 43947, August 1987.

Bruner, Jerome S. and Postman, Leo. 'Perception, cognition, and behavior.' *Journal of Personality*, September 1949, pp. 14–31.

Bradford, David L. and Cohen, Allan R. *Managing for Excellence*. New York: John Wiley & Sons, 1984.

Bruner, Jerome S. and Postman, Leo. 'On the perceptions of incongruity: a paradigm.' *Journal of Personality*, 1949, pp. 206–23.

Bruner, Jerome. *Actual Minds, Possible Worlds*. Cambridge, MA: Harvard University Press, 1986.

Bruner, Jerome. *On Knowing*. Cambridge, MA: Belknap Press, 1979.

Carroll, Lewis. *Alice's Adventures in Wonderland* and *Through the Looking-Glass and What Alice Found There*. Oxford: Oxford University Press, 1971.

Doody, Alton F. and Bingaman, Ron. *Reinventing the Wheels*. Cambridge, MA: Ballinger Publishing Company, 1988.

Furchgott, Roy. 'Surfing for satisfaction: consumer complaints go on line.' *The New York Times*, 8 June 1997, p. F8.

Gilovich, Thomas. *How What We Know Isn't So*. New York: The Free Press, 1991.

Grothe, Mardy and Wylie, Peter. *Problem Bosses*. New York: Ballantine Books, 1987.

Halberstam, David. *The Reckoning*. New York: Avon Books, 1986.

Hamermesh, Richard G. *Fad-Free Management*. Santa Monica, CA: Knowledge Exchange, 1996.

Iacocca, Lee. *Iacocca*. New York: Bantam Books, 1984.

Ingrassia, Paul and White, Joseph B. 'With its market share sliding, GM scrambles to avoid a calamity.' *The Wall Street Journal*, 14 December 1989, p. Al.

Jones, Malcolm Jr. 'Fields' genius made an art form out of lying.' *Newsweek*, 13 October 1997, p. 76.

Keller, Maryann *Rude Awakening*. New York: William Morrow and Company, Inc., 1989.

Kuhn, Thomas. *The Structure of Scientific Revolutions* (2nd edn, enlarged). Chicago, IL: University of Chicago Press, 1970.

Lublin, Joann S. 'Dear boss: I'd rather not tell you my name, but ...' *The Wall Street Journal*, 18 June 1997, pp. B1, B15.

Rodger, Will. 'Corporate threat: attack of the slamming sites.' *Inter@ctive Week*, 22 July 1996, pp. 18, 22.

Wensberg, Peter C. *Land's Polaroid*. Boston, MA: Houghton Mifflin, 1987.

'Next time, what say we boil a consultant.' *Fast Company*, November 1995, p. 20.

Report to the President by the U.S. Presidential Commission on the Space Shuttle Challenger Accident. Washington, DC, 1986.

Sin #7

Bart, Peter. 'How Sony became tony amid corporate convulsions.' *Daily Variety*, 28 July 1997, p. 22.

Boyd, John R. *A Discourse on Winning and Losing*. Air University Library, Maxwell Air Force Base, Report no. MU 43947, August 1987.

Catton, Bruce. *The Civil War*. New York: The American Heritage Library, 1960, 1988.

Deutsch, Claudia H. 'Asking workers what they think.' *The New York Times*, 22 April 1990, Section 3, part 2, p. 29.

Feynman, Richard P. 'An outsider's inside view of the Challenger Inquiry.' *Physics Today*, February 1988, pp. 26–37.

Gardner, Martin, ed. *The Annotated Alice*. New American Library, New York, 1960.

Gittler, Harvey. 'Well, shut my mouth ... please.' *The Wall Street Journal*, 9 January 1989.

Hammersmith, Richard G. *Fad-Free Management*. Santa Monica, CA: Knowledge Exchange, 1996.

Hirschman, Albert O. *Exit, Voice, and Loyalty*. Cambridge, MA: Harvard University Press, 1970.

Kendall, C.L. and Russ, Frederick A. 'Warranty and complaint policies: an opportunity for marketing management.' *Journal of Marketing*, April 1975, pp. 36–43.

Lele, Milind. *The Customer is Key*. New York: John Wiley & Sons, 1987.

Los Angeles Times. 'Timeless lessons of war found on a Civil War battlefield.' *The Boston Globe*, 10 August 1997, p. A21.

Mitchner, Brandon. 'J. D. Power's shadow looms over Europe.'

The Wall Street Journal, 27 June 1997, p. B9A.

Nielsen Researcher, No. 1, 1974, pp. 12–13.

Schoenfeld, Gabriel. 'Spy vs. Spy.' *The Wall Street Journal*, 27 August 1997, p. A10; review of Murphy, David E., Kondrashev, Sergei, and Bailey, George. *Battleground Berlin*. New Haven, CT: Yale University Press, 1997.

Simon, M.K., Omura, J.K., and Levitt, B.K. *Spread Spectrum Communications*. Rockville, MD: Computer Science Press, 1985.

Yankelovich, Daniel; Zetterberg, Hans; Strumpel, Burkhard; Shanks, Michael; Immerwahr, John; Noelle-Neumann, Elisabeth; Sengoku, Tamotsu; and Yuchtman-Yaar, Ephraim. *The World at Work: An International Report on Jobs, Productivity, and Human Values*. New York: Octagon Books, 1985.

Conclusion

Associated Press. ' '91 MIT report cited alcohol abuse.' *The Boston Globe*, 4 October 1997, p. B2.

Barnett, Donald F. and Crandall, Robert W. *Up From the Ashes*. Washington, DC: The Brookings Institution, 1986.

Barnett, Donald F. and Schorsch, Louis. *Steel: Upheaval in a Basic Industry*. Cambridge, MA: Ballinger Publishing Company1983.

Bickelhaupt, Susan and Dezell, Maureen. 'Seinfeld's "Soup Nazi" wins super Zagat honors.' *The Boston Globe*, 11 November 1997, p. E2.

Chacón, Richard. 'Students warned MIT on drinking.' *The Boston Globe*, 1 October 1997, pp. A1, A6.

Jenkins, Holman W. Jr. 'Turns out the year 2000 problem is just the beginning.' *The Wall Street Journal*, 6 May 1997, p. A23.

Kaplan, Red. 'Cream and punishment.' *The Boston Globe*, 22 November 1995, p. A3.

Lambert, Craig. 'Troubled book publishing: high type culture.' *Harvard Magazine*, November–December 1997, pp. 38 ff.

Milbank, Dana. 'Big steel is threatened by low-cost rivals, even in

Japan, Korea.' *The Wall Street Journal*, 2 February 1993, p. A1, A8.

Scism, Leslie and Paltrow, Scot J. 'Prudential's auditors gave early warnings about sales abuses.' *The Wall Street Journal*, 7 August 1997, pp. A1, A4.

White, David. 'Mondragón helps itself to success.' *Financial Times*, 10 June 1997, p. 25.

Index